FROM NEW RECRUIT TO HIGH FLYER

No-nonsense advice on how to fast track your career

Hugh Karseras

D1353177

KOGAN
PAGE

London and Philadelphia

This book draws on the contributions of hundreds of executives who between them have worked for over a hundred of the world's best-known organizations (see Appendix II) in first-rung roles. All individual executives are referred to with disguised names, but the organizations cited are real.[1] All views portrayed by these executives represent only the views of each individual not the organizations where they have worked.

Publisher's note

Every possible effort has been made to ensure that the information contained in this book is accurate at the time of going to press, and the publishers and author cannot accept responsibility for any errors or omissions, however caused. No responsibility for loss or damage occasioned to any person acting, or refraining from action, as a result of the material in this publication can be accepted by the editor, the publisher or the author.

First published in Great Britain and the United States in 2006 by Kogan Page Limited
Reprinted 2007

Apart from any fair dealing for the purposes of research or private study, or criticism or review, as permitted under the Copyright, Designs and Patents Act 1988, this publication may only be reproduced, stored or transmitted, in any form or by any means, with the prior permission in writing of the publishers, or in the case of reprographic reproduction in accordance with the terms and licences issued by the CLA. Enquiries concerning reproduction outside these terms should be sent to the publishers at the undermentioned addresses:

120 Pentonville Road
London N1 9JN
United Kingdom
www.kogan-page.co.uk

525 South 4th Street, #241
Philadelphia PA 19147
USA

© Hugh PA Karseras, 2006

The right of Hugh PA Karseras to be identified as the author of this work has been asserted by him in accordance with the Copyright, Designs and Patents Act 1988.

ISBN-10   0 7494 4564 5
ISBN-13   978 0 7494 4564 5

British Library Cataloguing-in-Publication Data

A CIP record for this book is available from the British Library.

Library of Congress Cataloging-in-Publication Data

Karseras, Hugh.
    From new recruit to high flyer : no-nonsense advice on how to fast track your career / Hugh Karseras.
       p. cm.
    ISBN 0-7494-4564-5
    1. Career development. 2. Executive ability. 3. Promotions. I. Title.

HF5381.K3645 2006
650.14—dc22

                                        2006018264

Typeset by JS Typesetting Ltd, Porthcawl, Mid Glamorgan
Printed and bound in Great Britain by Creative Print and Design (Wales), Ebbw Vale

[1] Some of these companies no longer exist today because of mergers, acquisitions etc.

Contents

About the author

Hugh Karseras began his career as an investment banking analyst with Deutsche Morgan Grenfell in London. Prior to his current position, he worked for management consultants McKinsey & Company, where he held the position of manager. He holds a degree *cum laude* in chemistry from Princeton University and an MBA from Harvard Business School. He currently lives in London with his wife, where he has recently begun working for another major investment bank.

Acknowledgements

This book would not have been possible without the generous contribution of hundreds of executives whom I feel genuinely privileged to count as friends as well as classmates and colleagues. I would like to thank all of you who contributed, through the online survey, structured interviews, casual conversations or e-mail exchanges.

Certain individuals are worthy of special thanks for going above and beyond in their support for this book. Matt Thomson has spent the most time with me, acting as an adviser, editor and contributor all in one. Oliver Backhouse and Mike Meyer have also spent more time with me than I deserve as both advisers and contributors. Yvonne Chien deserves special thanks for allowing me use of her company's 'Brainjuicer' technology to conduct the survey online and for her many thoughts on the subject matter. David Charters and Steve McCauley both deserve mention for providing the impetus to get this whole project off the ground and for offering truly pre-eminent advice.

I would also like to thank my agent, Simon Benham, for arriving on the scene with publisher in hand, and Jon Finch, Pauline Goodwin and everyone at Kogan Page for their generous support of this book.

Finally, I would like to thank my wife, Hayley, for her unerring love, support and patience, particularly in those early mornings, late nights and weekends that I spent working on the manuscript, and also for her keen eye for grammatical and typographical errors!

Introduction

It is over eight years since I first walked through those revolving doors on Bishopsgate in the financial square mile of London. I had finally made it through the gruelling circuit of interviews and was about to embark on my very first job, an entry-level graduate programme at a major investment bank. The career ladder stood before me, and this was the first rung.

I made my way, my knees a little wobbly and throat a little dry, to a large meeting room on the 19th floor where I joined 25 other new recruits. Shortly after, one of the senior directors kicked off the day talking about the history of the firm, the kind of work we would be doing and how exciting an opportunity this was for us. He continued by telling us that, for each one of us sitting in our seats, there were at least a hundred applicants who had been turned down. The part of the speech that I remember most vividly was when he warned us that in two years many of us would no longer be with the bank. Some, he explained, would leave of their own volition; others would be asked to leave.

I remember looking around at my peers and, like Tom Cruise's character, Maverick, in the film *Top Gun*, wondering who was the best. They were an impressive lot, mostly graduates of Oxford and Cambridge. They ranged from the quiet mathematics whizz-kid who was bound to be an ace at financial modelling, to one particularly self-confident and articulate Oxford graduate who was certain to impress the directors, to the army captain who seemed to ooze charm and charisma and was surely going to be a winner in front of clients. There were Master's degree and PhD graduates and even some who had worked for a couple of years in finance.

It turned out that those initial impressions of my peers were poor indicators of who ultimately succeeded. The mathematics whizz-kid did fine but was not much

> I remember looking around at my peers and, like Tom Cruise's character, Maverick, in the film *Top Gun*, wondering who was the best.

of a people person; the self-confident and articulate Oxford-educated graduate actually suffered for his haughty attitude; the army captain's charm and charisma were not enough to compensate for a questionable work ethic; and, for another executive, an insane work ethic was not able to compensate for poor communication skills.

If these talented individuals failed to be successful on the first rung, what then is required? Is it not simply a case of 'show up at work, do a good job and go home at the end of the day'? The bad news is that it is not that simple.

> *From New Recruit to High Flyer* is the result of in-depth research into the key success factors in entry-level jobs.

A guide to succeeding on the first rung of the career ladder

When I reflect on the start to my career, I am amazed at how little I knew. As I went through the job-hunting experience, I bought books on how to write cover letters and CVs and on how to do interviews. I am sure that many of you have done the same. I remember there being so many different books on interviewing, in particular, but not once did I come across a book that actually talked about what to do once you landed that first job. Of course, I read management books by people like Lee Iacocca (the famous turnaround CEO of Chrysler) and Mark McCormack (founder of IMG, the world's largest sports and talent agency), but these were books about top management that offered only limited early-career advice. What I really needed was a book that laid out the way to succeed specifically for someone starting out in their career, not for someone about to run a Fortune 500 company. I needed a book that was practical and to the point, and that contained the more pragmatic, smaller-picture tips, nuggets of advice and rules of thumb as well as the big-picture, philosophical advice. The book I wanted to read is the one I have written, and I know that I would have benefited enormously from the advice it contains.

From New Recruit to High Flyer is the result of in-depth research into the key success factors in entry-level jobs. It is based on the examination of the careers to date of hundreds of high-flying young executives from a broad cross-section of the world's best-known organizations. These individuals were top-of-the-class performers when they were entry-level; most of them are graduates of Harvard Business School and have gone on to continued rapid promotion or to new positions at some of the most selective companies in the world. Many of them are embarking on the middle rung of their career and now manage employees starting out on the first rung. Through this book, they have shared their thoughts on what made them and those around them successful. They have provided real-life examples from their own experiences on what made the difference for them when they were on the first rung and have also shared their perspectives on why their colleagues, who were often equally capable, were less successful. Most crucially, this book describes what you, as someone on the first rung, can do to learn from their collective experiences. I hope you will find it a practical and pragmatic guide to succeeding on the first rung of the career ladder.

Do you really need a guide to succeed on the first rung? Absolutely. One of the key lessons from my own experience was validated by the research, which showed how few of these high-flying young executives felt they knew what it took to succeed when they were on the first rung. They confirm that understanding the elements of success and how to apply those elements would have made them more effective more quickly, earned them more money and made their life a lot easier. For most, however, it is not so much a matter of making their journey to becoming successful easier; it is about the chance to become successful. The reality that emerges from the research is that those who fail do so not because they are not innately good enough, but simply because they do not follow certain principles.

What success means, why you should care and what this book will do for you

Before we begin on our journey to becoming a successful first-runger, let's just take a moment to consider the answers to the following questions. What exactly does being successful on the first rung mean? Why should you care about being successful? What will you get out of this book?

Becoming a successful first-runger is more than just coping in your new job. If you are looking for a survival guide, you should find another book. Being successful on the first rung means becoming a high performer. It means becoming an invaluable asset to your employer. It means making your bosses aware of your performance so that they are compelled to reward you. It means being the best.

Why should you care about being successful? There are several potential benefits, but most of the people surveyed for *From New Recruit to High Flyer* describe one or more of three main broad benefits:

1. **Higher pay and faster promotion.** Most established organizations now employ performance-related pay and promotion systems. Even on the first rung, typically at least 10 per cent of your annual salary is paid as an additional performance-related bonus. In service-oriented industries, eg banking and consulting, the bonus can even reach over 100 per cent of salary by the second year of employment. Similarly, promotion decisions are increasingly dependent on performance. Obviously, faster promotion also means higher pay as well as greater responsibility and authority.

2. **Better learning experience.** Even within a single entry-level programme, new employees often have markedly different experiences from each other. One may work on a dull, low-ranking project in the accounts department with an uninspiring boss while another may be part of a fun team doing exciting, high-profile work on a major new product or service launch. Being successful increases your chances of getting on the best assignments and having a better learning experience.

3. **Greater job satisfaction.** While it may seem that more money, faster promotion and great assignments would be enough for significant job satisfaction (they certainly will not hurt), there is something deeper that comes from succeeding in your job. It is about waking up every day and going to a place where you feel genuinely valued, where you feel a part of something and where you actually feel as though you belong. While it is important that you are pursuing the right career for you, regardless of where you are, you just cannot feel this deeper satisfaction if you are not succeeding.

So what will you get out of this book? You will gain an insider view of what organizations expect from their first-rung employees from those who have been there. You will develop an understanding of what it takes to succeed on the first rung from those who have been the most successful. You will read clear, practical and straightforward advice illustrated with real examples on how you can become a truly successful first-runger. If you have lofty aspirations and want to succeed (as I suspect you do if you have read this far), then this book will help you.

Overview of *From New Recruit to High Flyer*

From New Recruit to High Flyer is divided into three parts. Part 1 is focused on attitude. It is a single chapter, and it is the first chapter because above all else your attitude is the most important factor in determining your success. This fact is almost universally endorsed by all of the executives who contributed to this book. The key dimensions of attitude include a relentless work ethic, enthusiasm, a proactive and can-do approach, self-awareness and self-mastery.

Part 2 is the most practically oriented section of the book and includes many tips and pieces of advice that are immediately applicable to your day-to-day job. It focuses on how to develop the fundamental skills to succeed. These skills are a systematic approach; research and analysis; business communication skills; and project and people management skills specifically for first-rungers.

Part 3 looks at navigating the political organization, in particular your profile in it and your career path through it. With honed skills and the right attitude, you will be a high performer. Most organizations explicitly evaluate some form of these essential skills, attitudes and behaviours as part of performance reviews. However, even high performance does not necessarily translate into being truly successful. Despite the best efforts of many organizations to be fair in their performance review processes, there is no such thing as a genuinely meritocratic organization. High performance is not always recognized and rewarded; there are many other factors that come into play that are largely divorced from performance, eg office politics and personal prejudices. Part 3 is about taking control of your career beyond the scope of your day-to-day job and ensuring that you create the best opportunities for yourself, maximize your personal brand and ensure that those who matter fully recognize the impact of your work and contributions. Managing the organization involves three critical activities: building your network, finding your mentors and becoming politically savvy.

How to get the most out of *From New Recruit to High Flyer*

From New Recruit to High Flyer is more than just a book with a few ideas that will be helpful to you in your early career. In addition to offering lots of strategic advice to help you succeed in your career, it provides tips, tricks, rules of thumbs and tactical pieces of advice that are too numerous and specific to absorb in one reading. The best way to get the most out of this book is to:

1. read it once straight through to get an overview of the content;
2. read it through a second time with a pencil or highlighter and mark the text that you think offers the advice that is most useful to you personally;
3. refer back to the text frequently, checking in particular the text that you have marked and looking through the 'In a nutshell' summaries at the end of each chapter for a quick overview of the relevant pieces of advice;
4. reread the entire book after one year as a refresher.

Part 1

Attitude

1

It all starts with your attitude

If I had to write about only one thing, the one most important thing that determines success on the first rung, it would be attitude. In fact, of all the factors that hundreds of high-flying executives regarded as the most important, attitude clearly came out on top, with 70 per cent ranking it in the top category of importance and 97 per cent ranking it in the top two categories of importance. If the critical importance of attitude seems obvious to you, that is great, but the reality is that many young executives damage their chances of being successful because they do not have the right attitude. I warn you, though, do not expect to read this chapter and learn some fantastic easy answer to having the right attitude; getting your attitude right is hard and it is something you should not take lightly.

A boss of mine once told me about a review meeting where he and several senior managers were discussing the performance of a group of first-rung executives. They reviewed each executive in

> The reality is that many young executives damage their chances of being successful because they do not have the right attitude.

turn, initially by reviewing a written performance brief and then by discussing the opinions of those present in the room who had worked with the executive. For most of the executives reviewed, discussions were cordial and constructive, and, where a particular executive was deemed to be performing less well than expected, the senior managers tried to focus on areas where the executive could improve and develop.

One of the executives who came up for review was very bright and, in terms of the functional aspects of his job, everybody agreed that he was a high performer. However, a few of the senior managers made subtle noises about his overt 'brown-nosing', duplicity, arrogance and rudeness to peers and subordinates. One particular senior manager who had worked with this executive was more forthright. He interrupted the polite conversation and said: 'Look, let's cut to the chase here; the problem with him is that his attitude sucks – he is just a jerk!' There followed a brief silence as the group digested this statement, after which someone finally volunteered that, while this comment probably was not too far from the mark, it was not particularly helpful. This person asked the senior manager who had made the comment if he could suggest ways in which the executive could remedy his issues. The senior manager replied: 'Look, I'd love to give some more detailed comments, but sometimes, when you are dealing with a jerk, the only thing to say is: "Stop being a jerk!"'

It is a notion that brings to mind the words of the legendary General Electric CEO Jack Welch, who in a commencement ceremony at Harvard Business School in 2001 warned each member of the graduating class, 'Don't be a jerk!'

The story is a cautionary tale on two levels. Obviously, it serves to highlight the importance of attitude, but it should also warn you how hard it is to get your attitude right. The executive in the story was clearly highly motivated and talented. If you had asked him if he thought that he was a 'jerk', how do you think he would have responded? Of course, he would not have thought of himself as such. He may have had enough insight to recognize that he had behaved abrasively, even rudely on occasion, or appeared disrespectful or arrogant at times, but he would probably have put that down to 'having a bad day'. As Luke Patella of Bain & Company puts it: 'No one wakes up and decides: "Today, I am going to be a jerk!"'

You have to contend with a lot in life, and your professional career provides its own unique set of pressures and challenges. Sometimes it is difficult to work hard and be enthusiastic when you are tired or going through a tough period personally. Your own moods and reactions are naturally volatile, and you have to deal with others who are similarly subject to the same types of pressures, moods and reactions as you. With the best will in the world, it is not easy to sustain the best attitude and behaviours in the workplace all the time. But that is the challenge, and it is a critical challenge to meet, because attitude differentiates both positively and negatively; bosses appreciate a good attitude just as much as they dislike a bad attitude.

Why is attitude so important? The answer is the reason I am beginning this book with a chapter on attitude. It is because your attitude is the foundation for all the other attributes that you require to succeed. Your capacity to learn and perform the functional aspects of your job – the daily and ongoing tasks, your ability to communicate, your facility to work with people and your ability to build relationships and develop networks and mentors – all inexorably link to your attitude.

Of all the aspects of attitude that executives mention, the following themes recur time and time again and form the focus for this chapter.

Ensure a relentless work ethic

At the top of the list for attitude is your work ethic. Unprompted, over two-thirds of all the executives surveyed highlighted hard work as the number one ingredient for success. Think about that result for a second. If you know anything about marketing, you will know that an unprompted result of over two-thirds of a significant sample population is staggering. What is even more notable, however, is that even those who had been first-class honours students at superior universities or classic overachievers when they were growing up felt that hard work was the key.

The great news is that you do not need to be the most intelligent, in an academic sense, to succeed on the first rung. It is a cliché that B-grade students make better executives than A-grade students – because, so the argument goes, they are often more 'rounded'. Obviously, you must meet a threshold level of intelligence to succeed, but, above that threshold, additional intelligence does not usually make much difference.

So, if you think you can succeed with partial commitment, think again. There is no substitute for hard work and, let's be clear here, hard work is not only about working long hours; it is born of a deep desire to get your work done to the highest quality and in a timely fashion.

Bill Winters of Aerospace Industries, and David Cunningham of Goldman Sachs use the word 'relentless'. They argue that

> If you think you can succeed with partial commitment, think again.

complete commitment – a 'relentless work ethic' devoted to getting the job done, done on time and done well – is essential. They believe that you have to accept zero excuses for failing to fulfil what is asked of you if you want to deliver consistently high-quality end products and always be valuable to your boss and employer.

Steven Bond of Ralph Lauren believes that your commitment comes from 'a passion for what you are doing'. He says that it is much easier to work hard if you have an affinity with your job and career trajectory. In fact, a number of executives changed jobs very early on in their career in order to find a position where they enjoyed what they were doing. They knew that they would lose motivation quickly if they were not intrinsically interested by the nature or content of their job.

However, even if you love your job, do not be fooled into thinking that every day is going to be motivating. All executives mention times when they did not feel like putting in the hard work, staying late or focusing that extra attention on final quality control, even though in the big picture they loved their jobs. Sometimes, you have to complete some tedious or mindless assignment when you would rather be somewhere else. It is in these situations that the best executives demonstrate discipline and get on with the task in hand. As Harriet Giggs of PricewaterhouseCoopers instructs, 'Put your head down and get on with it.'

Often, your commitment is best exhibited when you have to sacrifice your time by working late or over the weekend. Proving willingness to sacrifice personal time is where many young executives fall down. There is a line to draw, but executives who show a lack of willingness to stay late when a project is in a critical phase quickly lose favour with their superiors.

Some executives, particularly those working in investment banks, highlighted the importance of 'face time', which they described as staying late, even when there was nothing to do, in order to be *seen* to be working hard. The game of face time can become farcical; I have seen some executives timing voicemails and e-mails to prove that they were working late, even though the e-mail or voicemail could perfectly well have gone out the next day. In certain environments, investment banking being an example, it is true that you will suffer if you are seen to leave earlier than your colleagues, but you have to be very careful about face time; in many companies, always staying late without doing work of any discernible value will only serve to classify you as unproductive.

Be enthusiastic and do not complain

Bosses and colleagues value enthusiasm. Enthusiastic people are likeable and fun to be around and they infect everyone with their energy; they contribute to an upbeat environment and make going to work more enjoyable. Some people naturally have a sunny disposition, while others do not, but regardless of your natural mood you have to learn to project enthusiasm. As Luke Patella of Bain & Company puts it: 'People gravitate towards people who are happy.'

Regardless of your natural mood or disposition, if you are in the right job you should have some enthusiasm for it. If you are not naturally enthusiastic about at least some part of the job, then it raises serious questions as to why you are where you are. It comes back to the importance of passion, as Stephen Bond of Ralph Lauren identified.

Before you think about actually projecting enthusiasm, a great place to start is to ensure that you never complain. You have to be disciplined here, because in the workplace, as in life, you frequently have justifiable cause to complain about something – that life is not fair should be nothing new. Nevertheless, the reality is that there is little that irks bosses and colleagues more than people who moan about their working situation, no matter how justified that may be. Even if they understand your situation, bosses hate any hint of bad morale, and if you openly express or exhibit dissatisfaction you will generally lose standing. It is that simple.

Jonathon Davies of Deloitte Consulting recalls an out-of-town project that everyone had tried to avoid; the project required the

> There is little that irks bosses and colleagues more than people who moan about their working situation.

team to spend five days a week in the middle of nowhere working on some pretty dull IT infrastructure implementation. At the 'kick-off' meeting, where the objective was to get everyone up to speed on the project, one first-runger, fresh from college, asked questions such as how long the project was going to last, what the lifestyle expectations were and how often he could go home mid-week. In other words, he showed little interest in the project itself but clearly communicated that he did not really want to be there.

Jonathon recalls the partner in charge of the project after the meeting expressing disgust at this first-runger's questions, not only because they were thinly veiled complaints and demonstrated a bad attitude, but because they also indicated poor judgement; the first-runger lacked the insight to recognize that he had thoroughly annoyed the partner, who would ultimately evaluate him and have significant input into his future prospects.

Did this first-runger have cause to complain? Absolutely! Who wants to be away from home every week for months on a terrible project in the middle of nowhere? But that is not the point. The thing about hard work is that it *is* hard! Sometimes it is hard because you have to commit long hours, sometimes because you have to work on something really difficult or boring, and other times because you have to work in an environment that may be unpleasant – a bad boss, uncooperative colleagues or a remote, boring location. While commitment will help you deliver on your assigned objectives, it is not enough without enthusiasm. You must maintain and project enthusiasm at all times.

In fact, Jonathon turned his peers' attitude towards the project to his advantage. He was one of the few executives who signed up to the project, because he recognized that he would get even more credit for his commitment and enthusiasm, which contrasted so distinctly with the others' lack of enthusiasm. Jonathon was rapidly promoted through the ranks and went on to become the top manager in his office.

Obviously, if you are being harassed, or your phone does not get fixed for two days, then you should complain in the appropriate way. As long as your focus is on trying to get on with doing good work, professionally made complaints will be well received.

Bill Winters of Aerospace Industries makes an additional point. You need to separate your personal life from your professional life. You may be having a shocking time at home: your girlfriend or boyfriend might have just left you; you might have had a huge fight with your parents; you might have crashed your car – it does not matter. As Bill puts it, 'Do not air your dirty laundry at work.' If something serious has occurred, such as bereavement in your immediate family, then you need to bring it up; but do so explicitly and through the appropriate channel (your direct boss usually), not implicitly through abnormal and unpredictable depressed behaviour.

If you do not complain, you will largely avoid creating a perception that you are unenthusiastic. But how do you go from 'not being unenthusiastic' to actually 'being enthusiastic', even when you have little appetite for a particular project? I do not like having to give the following advice, but I am convinced through my research and personal experience that in this particular case it is absolutely correct. Sometimes you have to fake it. If you find it impossible to be genuinely enthusiastic about a project or a piece of work and you cannot legitimately avoid it without upsetting anyone, you are better off pretending that you are enthusiastic. No one expects you to pretend that an unpleasant assignment is the best in the world, but they do expect you to put on a brave face. As one former first-runger who is now a manager puts it, 'There is nothing I like more than hearing the answer "Great" when I ask a junior guy, who I know is getting crushed, how they are getting on.'

Paul Graham of Wasserstein Perella & Co learned to 'wear a smile' no matter how terrible an assignment his boss gave him. David Bruce of Aramark agrees with this approach. He argues that bosses often realize exactly how unattractive a project is and they have nothing but respect for first-rungers who willingly adopt a 'taking one for the team' attitude. Such first-rungers not only demonstrate character strength by having mastery over their natural feelings, but they show their awareness of their role and position in the organization.

> No one expects you to pretend that an unpleasant assignment is the best in the world, but they do expect you to put on a brave face.

The poet Alfred, Lord Tennyson, in his famous tribute to the doomed charge of the Light Brigade in the Crimean War, wrote of the cavalry: 'Theirs not to make reply, Theirs not to reason why, Theirs but to do and die.' While giving up your life is probably going a little too far, you need to recognize that you are ultimately employed to work whether you like it or not, and even if you do not like it you are expected to be positive about it.

Adopt a genuinely proactive and can-do approach

One of the most common pieces of feedback that executives receive at every stage of the career curve is that they are not proactive enough. In some cases, the reason this feedback is given, particularly at review time, is that many firms require managers to identify 'weaknesses' or, in corporate-speak, 'areas for improvement' as well as to recognize strengths. 'You need to be more proactive' is such an easy 'improvement area' to suggest because it is so non-specific and the bounds of what constitutes proactivity are so ill defined. In the absence of any other real weaknesses, evaluators default to identifying proactivity as an issue.

Nevertheless, being proactive is important. Put yourself in the position of your boss for a moment. Imagine that the only way you can get your junior staff to do anything is by telling them, and then by repeatedly following up to make sure progress meets the schedule. You are going to have to spend a lot of time thinking about and explaining to subordinates what needs to be done and then monitoring progress. This time could be better spent elsewhere and, since you still have other work to do, you end up working extra hard. Would you not prefer your staff to be more autonomous and identify what needs to be done and get on with it? Would you not like your staff to come to you to keep you informed of progress? Would you not appreciate it if your staff actually came to you with ideas for work that they could get on with themselves and that would contribute to the performance of your group? Of course you would. Now return to being a first-runger, and you can see why being proactive is important.

Mary Peters of Microsoft believes that the exercise we went through above is the kind of exercise you should go through daily to be proactive. By putting yourself in your boss's shoes and thinking about what is important to him or her (for a good boss, this will be the same as what is important for your organization), you can anticipate the boss's needs and contribute without having to be told and without restricting yourself to a narrow job definition. Obviously, you have to be mindful of not overstepping the mark, but, as Luis Costa of Procter & Gamble suggests, you can avoid this mistake by running by your boss any ideas or projects you think you could undertake.

Closely allied to enthusiasm and a proactive approach is a 'can-do' attitude. Many first-rungers find all kinds of reasons why something cannot be done or why the project is a bad idea. You too will face a number of instances where you are asked to do a project that seems at the outset impossible and way beyond your capabilities or completely ridiculous. It is natural that first-rungers baulk when faced with such daunting projects, but by so doing they frustrate their boss with their negativity and ultimately destroy their boss's confidence. I have often heard a boss say 'I want solutions not problems' when an executive has flinched at a difficult project. Another common expression used by bosses that some executives mentioned is: 'Make it happen.'

You must instil confidence in your boss, not destroy it. No one expects you to solve the world's greatest problems on your own, but they do expect you to be good at finding a way to get the job done,

even if you do not know how
at the outset. As Carl Moran of
General Electric argues, you have
to remember that you are working
in a firm with a set of resources at
your disposal and usually, if you

No one expects you to solve the
world's greatest problems on your
own, but they do expect you to be
good at finding a way to get the
job done.

seek support from colleagues or talk to people who have done similar
projects before, or even ask for some help, you will get there.

Be flexible and helpful

Another big mistake that many first-rungers make when they start
their careers is to be too inflexible or, even worse, 'high and mighty'
about their roles. They set boundaries on what their job entails and
do not countenance helping beyond those boundaries, particularly if
helping includes menial tasks such as answering phones, photocopying
or carrying boxes etc. As Dan Barker of US Robotics describes it, some
first-rungers act as if they work in a union that dictates the precise
activities that its members do and do not undertake in each specific
type of job. In fairness, the recruiting departments of companies are
part of the problem. Because their goal is to attract good people to
their companies, they paint the most appealing picture of entry-level
jobs, focusing on the high level of responsibilities, exciting projects
and senior exposure that their company offers. They forget to mention
that the positions are at the bottom of the ladder and that recruits are
expected to perform all kind of unexciting tasks and work on some dull
projects because someone has to do the work. MBA graduates are often
most guilty of the 'high and mighty' problem, because they come from
a business school environment that often makes its students feel too
self-important.

Jonathon Davies of Deloitte Consulting remembers a team meeting
at a critical stage of a project where the team had to prepare a large
number of documents for an urgent and imminent deadline. When the
partner leading the project asked a second-year analyst on the team to
help staple the documents, the analyst replied that his job was not to
staple documents and that support staff should do that kind of work.
The partner did the stapling himself, providing no better proof that
stapling is not just for support staff. Because he was uncooperative, the
analyst destroyed, in a single minute, his relationship with that partner,

who could have proved a powerful advocate and ally in his future career.

If someone needs you to carry boxes, carry the boxes. If your team needs photocopying, head to the photocopying room. If you need to spend a day keying in data to a database, get to it. Often, you will find that you have assistants and support staff who will take care of these things for you, but you should not view any task as beneath you. Often, it is in the biggest crunches that helping on the menial tasks is when it matters most. As Jack Reardon of American Medical Security puts it: 'Sometimes, you must roll your sleeves up and be willing to get your hands dirty.'

Ultimately, you have to want to be helpful, no matter what it entails. Florence Elias of NBC used to answer the phone and take messages for her boss. Whenever she went out for coffee, she would bring an extra one back. She did not care that these were 'menial duties'; she knew that she was helping her boss and that she did not lose anything herself by helping. She had the right mindset, and it was an important factor in her continuing successful career, where she is now an executive producer.

Develop a deep-seated desire to learn

In the next few chapters, we cover the main kinds of tasks that you will face on the first rung. In Chapter 2, one section focuses on how to 'Get smart at getting smart'. It discusses tactics and strategies for climbing the learning curve as fast as possible. However, without a deep-seated desire to learn, these tactics and strategies are of little use.

A deep-seated desire to learn is important on two levels. Most obviously, you need to master your job and all the activities that it entails. More subtly, however, you also need to demonstrate an ability to climb the learning curve as fast as possible. You need to convince your bosses not only that you are very capable in your current job but also that you can grow quickly into a new role with new responsibilities.

As you move up the career ladder, you will discover that some of the best opportunities to progress do not arise from moving through a structured career path with standard tenure-linked promotions, but serendipitously, because someone leaves or the business grows into new products and new geographies. When such personnel gaps arise, rarely can bosses identify a clear candidate for a new role. Instead they look to employees whom they think would be able to learn how to handle the role most quickly and most effectively. If they cannot find internal candidates, they recruit externally.

Adrian White of United Health Insurance believes that you must develop inquisitiveness. In his own job, particularly when he was assigned to a new and unfamiliar project, he would ask question after question to get up to speed as fast as possible. Jack Reardon of American Medical Security agrees; he was known by the nickname 'Quick Question' because he frequently used to stop by his colleagues' and bosses' offices with a quick question on some or other issue. Chris Moritz of Teligent states it differently, however; he argues that a complete 'commitment to mastery' underpins excellence.

Ultimately, it does not matter what drives your deep-seated desire to learn – whether it is the act of learning that inspires you, or the sense of accomplishment that

> Sometimes, you must roll your sleeves up and be willing to get your hands dirty.

comes from mastery. It just matters that you have the desire to learn and improve.

Be humble and show honest respect

Too many first-rungers start off their careers lacking humility and they do not demonstrate enough respect to their colleagues, their seniors or, worst of all, the administrative and support staff. Often, the problem is greatest with the more talented first-rungers. Typically, they have been high flyers at school or university and are used to accolades and being elite. Suddenly, they enter the workforce and, although the career ladder stretches above them, they behave as if they were on the final rung of the ladder, not on the first rung. They are both expectant of rapid advancement and derisory of work that is 'beneath' them. Despite their intellectual calibre, they have completely missed the point.

If you have not picked it up yet, a lot of doing well is about handling people. There is nothing wrong with having self-confidence – on the contrary, self-confidence

> If you have not picked it up yet, a lot of doing well is about handling people.

is important – but, when it spills over into arrogance and disdain for others, it becomes a problem for the simple fact that people will not like you.

I have seen it in my own career a number of times. When I started out in investment banking, one of my fellow first-rungers was a very clever Oxford graduate. He had an air about him of everything and everyone boring him. Despite his obvious intellectual calibre, the senior managers regarded him poorly and he did not last long.

Within an attitude of respect and humbleness is a spirit of open-mindedness and recognition of the value of difference. Renee Jordan of Ford notes that the workplace is often a melting pot for people from all walks of life and that it is important that you value their differences and potentially alternative perspectives and make them feel that you value them.

Exhibit a contagious team spirit

The ability to work in teams is mentioned in almost every single recruiting brochure you will ever read, and it is indeed a critical dimension of any successful first-runger's attitudinal make-up. The reason team spirit is so important is because, as Christy Roberts of Intuit put it, one question that a lot of people ask is: 'Would I want to work with this person again?' Ensuring that people want to work with you again goes beyond likeability and enthusiasm; you need to have team spirit, a sense of collaboration and a willingness to subordinate yourself to the needs of the team.

> One question that a lot of people ask is: 'Would I want to work with this person again?'

Learn self-awareness and self-mastery

This opening chapter contains common-sense thoughts on attitude. I do not expect you to be surprised by its contents, but I do expect you to take it very seriously, for two reasons:

1. You need to appreciate how important attitude is to your success.
2. You need to recognize how very hard attitude is to get right.

It is truly difficult and you will repeatedly fail on a number of these critical attitudinal dimensions.

I once asked a senior partner at a major consulting firm, who over the course of his career had conducted hundreds of meetings with consultants whom the company had asked to leave as part of its 'up or out' programme, what the missing factor was in those consultants who did not make the grade. His answer was: 'A combination of self-awareness and self-mastery.'

Self-awareness is about understanding yourself, how you respond to different stimuli and how you behave in different environments. It is being honest about your strengths and weaknesses and facing up to what you have to change in yourself to achieve your goals. Self-mastery is about making those changes. It is hard, and requires real discipline and determination. Ultimately, a combination of self-awareness and self-mastery underpins all the attributes of attitude and the lessons in this book because it drives self-development and evolution. Nobody walks into any job with all the characteristics, behaviours and skills required to succeed; people have to learn and develop them, but those who do succeed do so because they are self-aware and are masters over themselves.

> Those who succeed do so because they are self-aware and are masters over themselves.

Closing thoughts on attitude

Hopefully, the importance of attitude is clear to you by now. But I can imagine you thinking: 'Wait a second. This rounded, enthusiastic, respectful, be-nice approach is all well and good, but I know lots of people who aren't like this who do well – people like the one in that earlier review meeting story. They are arrogant and rude. How is it that these people do well? In fact, isn't the expression "Nice people finish last" truer?'

I have to concede that most organizations contain many people with poor attitudes, although I would remind you that few try to be like this. However, the one trait that these people typically possess is that they are all very hard workers. In other words, they have the most important attitudinal quality. Their style is very much focused on results. This is often why they are what they are to begin with. They are so intent on results and delivering high-quality work that everything else gets lost. Furthermore, when they are first-rungers, unlike the executive in the review meeting, they are also often very clever in that they make sure that they demonstrate the right attitude in front of their bosses and other senior decision makers. In other words, they manage their perception with those who matter (we discuss managing perception in Chapter 9). It is only when dealing with people whom they view as unimportant to their careers that they reveal their less palatable qualities. Personally, I think such individuals take a short-sighted approach. A career lasts a long time and I am a firm believer in people eventually being 'found out'.

Most importantly, though, is that, while a poor attitude does not preclude being highly successful, I believe – and most of the executives included in the research validate this belief – that your best chance of being successful does start with having the right attitude.

In a nutshell – How to have a great attitude

■ Ensure a relentless work ethic.

■ Be enthusiastic and do not complain.

■ Adopt a proactive and can-do approach.

■ Be flexible and helpful.

■ Develop a deep-seated desire to learn.

■ Be humble and show honest respect.

■ Exhibit a contagious team spirit.

■ Learn self-awareness and self-mastery.

Part 2

Master the fundamentals

2

Adopt a systematic approach

The best first-rungers are rarely rushed and are able to respond rapidly to the needs and demands of their jobs without undue stress and panic. They get more done in less time without any sacrifice in quality. They never lose files or documents and they have everything close at hand when they need it. As their roles change, they are always one step ahead of the curve and able to handle what is thrown at them. In short, they are supremely organized, extremely efficient managers of their time, and fast learners. The reason why the best first-rungers are so organized, manage their time so well and learn so quickly is because they all share two common traits: they are disciplined, and they are systematic in their approach to their job and their work. Developing a systematic approach to your job and your work is the focus of this chapter. When it comes down to it, being systematic in your approach is about guaranteeing consistent and high-quality results or, as George Malone of Goldman Sachs put it, 'it is about always delivering'.

This chapter is organized into three sections: the first section deals with the approach and habits that you require to be supremely organized; the second focuses entirely on efficient and effective time management; and the third section covers how to 'get smart at getting smart' – how to climb the learning curve rapidly.

> Being systematic in your approach is about guaranteeing consistent and high-quality results... it is about always delivering.

Developing supreme organizational skills

Being supremely organized is about building an infrastructure around you that facilitates consistent and efficient delivery of your work. This infrastructure begins with your physical work environment and extends to the way that you manage your computer and your paperwork. The rest of this section focuses on what you need to do to build and maintain this infrastructure.

Establish an efficient physical workspace

Most first-rungers do not have their own office. You can expect to have a desk in a cubicle, as part of an open-plan office, or in an office that you share with colleagues. Regardless of where you sit, you should ensure that you organize your desk so that there is always:

■ clear desk space so that you can write, edit or read through documents etc;

■ computer space neatly organized with sufficient space for keyboard and mouse;

■ a system of prioritizing action items, for example using in-trays for memos, documents etc;

■ a waste-paper basket nearby to bin immediately anything that is no longer needed;

■ a clock (you can use your computer if you wish) to ensure time-keeping;

■ essential stationery items, ideally in a stationery holder;

■ (if it is absolutely necessary) only neat piles of documents that do not impede the clear desk space.

Endeavour to keep your desk organized at all times. Not only will keeping an efficient physical workspace portray professionalism, organization and control, but it will also help you establish the right mindset to be professional and systematic.

Methodically file physical documents

You should establish a filing system that takes care of all the paperwork you have as a consequence of general administration, eg expenses, payslips, evaluation reports, travel documents and contact details. In addition, you should organize a set of files for your ongoing projects. Everyone has their own filing system, but you should ensure that your files are clearly labelled and organized logically in terms of what belongs in which file and in terms of the sequence of files, eg alphabetically or chronologically. The first measure of how methodically you file documents is how quickly you can retrieve any specific document. The second and more stringent measure is how quickly someone unfamiliar with your filing system can retrieve a specific document. As the most junior person on any team, you will be the most approachable person for documents, so expect to be asked for them and organize accordingly.

Methodically save and file electronic documents

As with filing physical documents, you will also need a methodical approach to saving and filing electronic documents. Electronic filing is more complex than physical filing because the number of files is typically far greater. Again, different people have different systems, but there are some common principles:

■ **Create a master folder.** You should save most of your files on your hard drive unless your organization has special network directories that you need to use. Either way, you need to set up a master folder that holds all of your work. If you are saving to your hard drive, this should be in 'My Documents' for Windows-based computers.

■ **Build a logical hierarchy of folder by subject.** Within your master folder you should organize your folders logically. I personally prefer to organize my folders by type of project. For example, when I was a banker, I learned to organize folders by deal or by marketing pitch. Sometimes, you may want folders dedicated to work that you do for individuals within your organization. Within each of these broad subject folders you should organize folders along the type of work; for example, you may have one folder dedicated to analysis, one folder dedicated to final deliverables, one folder dedicated to process, one folder dedicated to background documents etc. Again, the best measure of efficient filing is how quickly your colleagues are able to retrieve any given file.

The best measure of efficient filing is how quickly your colleagues are able to retrieve any given file.

■ **Apply consistent naming methodology for files.** Every file with a folder needs to be named. Many firms have their own convention for naming files, but the best that I have seen start with numerical dates in the order year, month, day, followed by a short, crisp description of the file. For example, the electronic file for this chapter is '050802 Chapter 2 – Adopt a systematic approach'. The advantage of this naming convention is that within a folder it sequences all files by date from oldest at the top to the newest files at the bottom.

■ **Always 'Save As' to the appropriate folder first.** When you open up a new document from within a programme and try to save it, the programme forces you to 'Save As' and to name the file. You need to do this every time you create a new document, and you need to make sure you save it to the right folder; otherwise you will have trouble finding the file later. In particular, one error that has caused a lot of frustration for many executives arises when people open up attachments directly from e-mails. Automatically, the computer creates a file in the temp folder, and when you hit 'Save' it only saves the latest version to the temp folder. When you shut down your computer, your temp folder empties and your work is lost. Develop the habit of never opening attachments from e-mail; instead 'Save As' to a folder and open from within the folder, and you will avoid this frustration.

■ **Use autosave or develop a 'Control S' tic.** A similarly frustrating experience that many first executives go through is losing work because their computer crashes. Either make your programs autosave or become obsessed with hitting Control S, the keystrokes to save your work in all Windows-based programs. If you choose the latter, you should habitually hit Control S every few minutes, as if you have a tic.

■ **Ensure version control.** Typically, any document that will have input from colleagues or other firms needs to go through many rounds of editing. Always have a single 'master' of the physical document that contains all of the latest handwritten edits. On the cover of the master, actually write 'master' and also the time and date. If you collect handwritten copies from multiple people on the same document, then consolidate the comments into your master. Keep all of your past masters until you have sign-off on the final version. The time and date will allow you to refer back to old edits, as is often required. Similarly, get into the habit of saving old electronic versions of documents; content that has been edited out of an old version all too frequently reappears in final documents. Your master should be the most recent file. If you have saved all of the original electronic versions, you can recover old content and save time and effort on duplication. The best approach to manage versions that I have encountered is to add 'V1', 'V2', 'V3' etc to the end of the document name. One approach I have personally found useful is to keep three folders for each piece of work: one folder that is for old versions; one that is for the current electronic 'master'; and one that is for signed-off final documents.

■ **Back up regularly.** Even if you save your work religiously, your hard drive is not immune to crashing completely. Many organizations force you to back up your files regularly. If they do not, you should make sure that you do so yourself. The best approach is to back up to your network, so that, if anything physically happens to your computer that destroys everything, or if you lose your laptop, you will always have access to your files.

Never go anywhere without these

You should always carry an extra pen, a notepad and a calculator whenever you go to any kind of meeting or to see a boss or colleague. If there is ever a requirement to do a quick calculation in

> Always carry an extra pen, a notepad and a calculator whenever you go to any kind of meeting or to see a boss or colleague.

a meeting, you should be ready to run the numbers there and then. I have seen bosses actually tell off first-rungers for not bringing a calculator to meetings. An extra pen is useful because your bosses will sometimes forget their own pen and will ask to use yours. Your notepad should also be with you at all times for reasons we discuss below. Make sure your name and contact number are on the cover of your notebook in case you leave it somewhere; you will have more chance of recovering it. Many executives tape their business cards on to the cover.

Keep thorough notes

Keeping notes is an essential part of the first-runger's job. In every meeting, even if there is a nominated scribe, you should keep your own notes. Whenever you receive instructions or tasks to perform, you should keep a clear log of exactly what you need to do, by when and any other relevant information such as leads or resources to leverage. Get into the habit of recording times and dates so that you can easily use your notes, and try to develop your own code that highlights, for example, critical information or tasks that you have to perform. One of the most important uses of a notepad is to keep 'to-do' lists, which we discuss in detail in the next section.

Becoming a highly efficient time manager

If there is one truism that hits home most frequently, it is that there is not enough time in the day. Twenty per cent of executives surveyed wished they had known more about how to be effective time managers before they began their career. In particular, they wished they had appreciated the importance of prioritization, a critical aspect of time management that we discuss in further detail below. One of the defining characteristics of the most effective first-rungers is their ability to make the most of the time that they have available and get more done, without any loss of quality, than their peers. The focus of this section is the tips and techniques the best executives adopt to manage their time most effectively.

> One of the defining characteristics of the most effective first-rungers is their ability to make the most of the time that they have available and get more done.

Make an early start

I am not an early riser. Far from it – I hate getting up in the morning, particularly on cold, dreary winter mornings, when the pillow is soft and the bed warm. In fact, for much of my early career I would always trade off in favour of getting more sleep, but I have learned that sometimes it is better to trade off in favour of less sleep – at least in the short term

– in order to get an early start on the day. This lesson is validated by the experience of a number of the executives interviewed.

Particularly when you have a lot of work and tight deadlines, you are far better off getting in early and getting a head start on your day. As Jack Reardon of American Medical Security argues, the early morning is often the most productive time because you are less interrupted by phone calls, e-mails and colleagues stopping by, and can focus on getting on with your real work.

Paul Graham of Wasserstein Perella & Co adds that getting an early start reduces your stress levels in the day because you feel more on top of your workload and less rushed. Paul even spends time on Sundays getting everything in order, so that he is able to begin the week feeling on top of things and with a clear view of what he has to achieve. Jeremy Smith of SmithKline Beecham points out that beating the morning rush on your way into work saves time on your commute, again adding to your overall productivity.

Plan ahead

When it comes to project management, planning ahead is vital. For example, if you do not plan ahead, you will not appreciate that some parts of the project that have later deadlines need to start before other parts with earlier deadlines either because they have longer lead and/ or cycle times (time they take to initiate or to complete) or because contingencies exist (other deadlines rely on their completion).

When it comes to time management, planning ahead is similarly important in order to manage your work flow and ensure that you deliver quality output. Essentially, planning ahead is about anticipating where you need to focus and explicitly scheduling your time up front.

> Planning ahead is about anticipating where you need to focus and explicitly scheduling your time up front.

Planning at some firms is built into the culture. For example, Luis Costa of Procter & Gamble recalls that his personal work plans emerged from a 'top-down' planning process that started at the beginning of the year for his whole group. His group initially created a long-term plan for the year that included major projects. At Procter & Gamble, these major projects typically related to management of a 'brand', such as a major washing powder. The group manager then distributed the projects among the team members.

The group captured these broad plans in a detailed Gantt chart (see 'Managing projects smoothly' in Chapter 6) incorporating the major milestones and indicating which team member was responsible for which projects. At the beginning of each month, the team members built a more detailed Gantt chart for the month, which adjusted for any changes in the overall year work plan. Finally, at the beginning of each week, each team member met with his or her boss, discussed projects and key tasks for the forthcoming week and reviewed the previous week's projects and key tasks to track progress and performance.

Not all firms use such a strict planning protocol as Procter & Gamble. Neither does planning have to be a science. Mike Sandler of McMaster-Carr describes a simpler approach to planning ahead, which achieves similar benefits:

> *I take a look at my calendar for the next few days and figure out what I need to accomplish and by when. This creates a plan for my next few days. With this plan, I can force myself to stay on task. I also avoid staying late every night because of not knowing when I will have another chance to work on a task, and I do not waste time during the day trying to figure out what I should be doing. My time is always spent working towards an accomplishment.*

Jim Taylor of Merrill Lynch agrees with Mike's approach and focuses on the importance of anticipation. As he puts it: 'If you work from behind, you have to react all day and you cannot provide as good an output as when you anticipate.' He adds: 'It gets hard to anticipate when you are running around putting out fires.'

If you work from behind, you have to react all day and you cannot provide as good an output as when you anticipate.

Use a diary

All computer programs have a program that serves as a calendar, although if you prefer to be 'old-school' you can use a written diary. Develop the habit of recording all your meetings and commitments in your diary. Early on in your career, you may be able to rely on memory for meetings, particularly if you do not have that many. However, as soon as meetings start to mount up, you run the risk of forgetting them or double-booking yourself. Many firms provide PDAs that synchronize with your computer and allow you to book meetings wherever you are. If you do not use a PDA, then record all meetings in your notebook and be sure to transfer them to your diary at the first opportunity.

Begin and end your day with to-do lists

To-do lists are among the most basic of time management tools but one of the most effective ways to manage your workload and day. Kirk Williams of Chrysler recommends that you begin every

> To-do lists are among the most basic of time management tools but one of the most effective ways to manage your workload and day.

day by writing a to-do list and ticking each item off or crossing it out as you complete each task. His goal is to cross off every single item on his list by the end of the day. Not only, he explains, does the to-do list focus your mind, but it also provides a sense of accomplishment and momentum throughout the day that further spurs your productivity.

To-do lists, though, should not replace work plans. Luis Costa of Procter & Gamble supports his detailed monthly and weekly work plans with to-do lists that he prepares at the beginning of each day. His to-do lists provide clarity around his immediate tasks and activities and ensure that his short-term focus is in line with the longer-term objectives of his monthly and weekly plans.

Jonathon Davies of Deloitte Consulting is also a big fan of to-do lists and recommends keeping an ongoing to-do list throughout the day, crossing off completed tasks, as Kirk Williams does, and adding to them when necessary.

Personally, the final thing that I do at the end of the day is to write my to-do list for the next day. At that time, I have the clearest view of remaining work and I feel a sense of closure for the day by mentally allocating any new tasks as the next day's work.

Learn to prioritize

One of the most apparent, and yet most poorly applied, principles of time management is prioritization. Most obviously, prioritization involves deciding what to do and what not to do, and how to sequence activities, in other words choosing which things to do first. Less obviously, however, prioritization is also about choosing where to expend most effort. While you should ensure that everything you produce is finished to professional quality, above this threshold there are still degrees of quality that you can flex when you prioritize.

When you think about prioritization the following three factors are the most important to take into account:

> Prioritization is also about choosing where to expend most effort.

■ **Deadlines.** Luis Costa of Procter & Gamble starts prioritization by looking at forthcoming deadlines. Knowing how much time it will take to hit each deadline, he sequences his tasks to make sure that he hits his deadline, taking into consideration how much time he needs to allow for pre-work preparation, how long it takes to complete the work, and contingencies, as we discuss in Chapter 6 as part of project management.

■ **Importance.** Carl Moran of General Electric prioritizes what he calls the 'boulders' first. These are the big pieces of work that matter most. If he delivers his best quality on these, he knows that he has taken care of the crux of his job and can then turn his attention to less critical tasks. Jack Reardon of American Medical Security makes the point that in order to prioritize you first need to understand clearly what 'matters most' – that is, what is most important to your boss and firm. Once you understand the 'pecking order' of tasks, you can decide which tasks demand your greatest efforts. Jack knows that he has to manage two broad types of task within his company: operational tasks and administrative tasks. Operational tasks are focused on revenue-related activities, while administrative tasks are internally focused and include things like recruiting and internal reporting. Jack knows that, all other things being equal, operational tasks come before administrative tasks and so he makes sure that he prioritizes them.

■ **Minimum time involved.** Sometimes, however, you should complete some tasks that are less important than others if they are quick to execute and would otherwise have to wait a long time before being completed if you were solely to focus on the most pressing pieces of work. This is particularly true if these little tasks involve getting back to people who are waiting for a response.

Jeremy Smith of SmithKline Beecham will respond to certain calls and certain e-mails before he undertakes the most important piece of work, because he knows the mileage that he gets out of responding to colleagues quickly. The trick here is not to let a hundred little things turn into a time sink – knock off a handful of the most important little tasks and put the rest to one side until you genuinely have time to run through them all.

Parallel processing

One of the most confusing mantras of the last couple of decades has been 'Learn to multi-task.' The image of someone typing away at a computer, while talking on the phone and, at the same time, holding a conversation with someone standing near, has come to epitomize the multi-tasker. The reality is that this image of multi-tasking encourages ineffective time management. The mind cannot simultaneously process more than one conscious thought at a time and so all that multi-tasking achieves is a dilution of focus on any one task because the mind is forced to switch back and forth between different activities in rapid succession. The result is sloppy work that requires rework later. Sometimes, multi-tasking is necessary, but do not confuse necessary overlaps in activities with effective time management. The real principle that drives the ability to manage more than one task at a time is parallel processing.

Similarly to multi-tasking, parallel processing means managing two or more processes at the same time (in parallel). The difference compared with multi-tasking is

> The real principle that drives the ability to manage more than one task at a time is parallel processing.

that parallel processing does not attempt to force you to think or actively do two or more things at the same time. How is this possible? One or both of two principal conditions make parallel processing possible. The first and most important is the ability to delegate. The second and less obvious comes back to lead times.

The importance of delegation is also covered in Chapter 6 on project management. The essence is as follows: with an investment of time up front and, if necessary, periodic monitoring and follow-up, finding someone else to pick up a piece of work for you, even if it is only typing up a memo, proofreading a document or finding some information, frees up time for you to work on something else.

If two activities have different lead times, you can also parallel-process them by starting the activity with the longer lead time first and then focusing your attention on the activity with the shorter lead time. For example, when Jeremy Smith of SmithKline Beecham arrives at his desk in the morning, the first thing he does is to switch on his computer. He knows it takes a couple of minutes to boot up, so he creates time to check voicemail messages or to make a start on his to-do list. Other less efficient executives see the flashing light on their phone and cannot help but deal with their voicemail before they do anything else, or they feel compelled to focus on their to-do lists as their very first activity.

Two of the parallel-processing opportunities I most commonly encounter are printing a long document or running a large download or a complex query from a database. By sending the document to print, or downloading the file or running the query well before I need them, I can get on with some other piece of work while printing or downloading. I avoid unproductive wait time. These examples of lead-time-linked parallel processing do not save anywhere near as much time as delegation, but little and frequent time-savers over the course of the day are often what make the difference between the efficient and inefficient time manager.

Learn the short cuts

The best time managers tend to be very efficient not only at how they organize and schedule activities but also at how they perform individual tasks that they cannot delegate. One of the secrets that they have learned is to take advantage of short cuts. Taking short cuts is not about being less thorough. It is about per- forming exactly the same task in a different and more efficient way. The following are key short-cut opportunities:

> Taking short cuts is not about being less thorough. It is about performing exactly the same task in a different and more efficient way.

■ **Leverage existing work.** One of the things you will quickly come to realize is that much duplicative work exists in even the most efficient organization. Usually, someone somewhere has already done something similar to the task that you have to do. Frequently, you can leverage materials and knowledge to give you a good head start. Even if it is only a phone call to someone who has experience of the task you are facing, it can save you hours and even days of heading down the wrong path. As Mike Sandler of McMaster-Carr puts it, 'Lots of smart people have walked your floors before; don't discover everything for yourself.' Even if you have a clear picture of how to perform a task, you are better off validating that approach beforehand, or if you were already on the right track you have validated your approach and given your work greater credibility as a consequence.

■ **Ask for help and direction early.** A major mistake that most first-rungers make is to be unwilling to ask for help and direction early for fear of appearing stupid or inexperienced. Do not let pride get in the way of your efficiency. Ask for help and direction, and ask early. As Dan Barker of US Robotics puts it, 'The time to ask for help is before you need it.'

■ **Learn to touch-type.** You will have to do a lot of typing in any first-rung job and, if you are a slow and cumbersome typist struggling to hit 20 words per minute compared with a proficient touch-typist hitting 50–60 words per minute, you will waste an enormous amount of time. If you are not already a proficient typist, go out now and buy a tutorial software package that will teach you.

■ **Stop using the mouse.** The amount of time that first-rungers have to spend locked to a computer means that efficient time management also means using your computer efficiently. Look at most inefficient computer users and you will see that they use the mouse constantly. They click on menus and point to parts of the screen. Over the course of the day, you spend a lot of time in front of a computer, and the time you take to point and click adds up to a significant total amount. Almost everything you can do with a mouse can be done directly with keystrokes. Most programs underline letters in all of their menus and, by holding down the 'Alt' key and hitting the underlined letter, you can access that menu. Even if you have to use three keystrokes to get to the right function, you will be quicker than by using the mouse. You will be surprised at how quickly you learn the keystroke sequences for multiple functions.

Do not procrastinate

One of the things that I have seen many executives struggle with is procrastination. Some executives seem to have a knack for finding all manner of time sappers to divert their attention – whether it is personal e-mail, a news website or a pressing need to reorganize their stationery drawer. The problem, they like to believe, is that they have a very short attention span and low tolerance for mundane activities. However, the reality is that there are all manner of boring tasks that one has to undertake, and even interesting tasks can be dull when repetitive. I have often walked into offices of peers and subordinates and seen them swiftly strike the 'Alt' and tab keys to switch programs from their favourite news website to some half-completed Word document. Not only do they come across as unproductive, but they look as if they have been caught red-handed. They are better off leaving the news website on and being open about taking a break.

What can you do to limit procrastination? When I asked executives this question, most were unsympathetic and said: 'Just get on with it.' There is a lot of truth in the 'Just get on with it' approach – sometimes there is no easy fix. Having said that, a few executives did offer some useful advice to help you control your procrastination tendencies.

What can you do to limit procrastination? When I asked executives this question, most were unsympathetic and said: 'Just get on with it.'

Carl Moran of General Electric suggests setting your own deadlines to focus on completing work without distraction. If you have to write a memo that will reasonably take an hour to complete, carve out one hour, commit to finishing the memo by the end of that hour and do not let anything unimportant distract you.

James Edwards of Novartis builds in explicit break time upon completion of certain tasks. As he puts it: 'Knowing that I have a break that is linked to completing a task makes me focus on getting that task completed as fast as possible. I do not procrastinate because then I feel less good about taking a real break.' This simple reward system is very effective at focusing the mind.

Touch simple items only once

One of the biggest inefficiencies in time management arises not just from duplication of effort within a firm, but by duplication of effort by single executives. Most executives tend to receive a lot of small requests throughout the day, such as making a phone call to a colleague to answer a quick question, forwarding a document or updating a boss on some project. When memos, e-mails and voicemails, all asking you to do these little things, bombard you and you are very busy, it is very tempting to open up the e-mails, look at the memos, listen to the voicemails and then put them to one side and revisit them later when you are under less pressure. This is a mistake. The duplicated effort of rereading e-mails or memos or of re-listening to voicemails adds up and translates to a meaningful drain on your time.

If you are busy with a piece of work, you are right not to take time out to perform a host of small tasks, but then the real questions are: if you are busy, why have you checked your voicemail, why have you opened your e-mail and why have you read the memo? The answer is that you should not have looked at them until you were ready to deal with them. Obviously, when urgent matters arise you need to respond, but if something is urgent you can normally tell from the e-mail subject header, and, rather than leaving a voicemail, people will always try to call you if the matter is truly urgent. As for memos, by their very nature these are rarely urgent.

As Mike Sandler of McMaster-Carr puts it: 'Touch each piece of paper, each e-mail, each voicemail etc once and only once.' Practically, what this means is that, if you open up an e-mail, for instance, which asks you to forward a document or to make a call, you should do it straight away and then delete or file the e-mail. Do not add it to your to-do list, or you will be wasting further time. Only if the e-mail, memo or voicemail demands a serious piece of work should you add it to your to-do list and then you should factor it into your schedule. As a rule of thumb, if you can respond in less than five minutes do it straight away; if it is going to take longer, schedule it in your work plan.

Getting smart at getting smart

While the successful young executives who contributed to this book highlighted lots of specific advice on how to perform the core and other aspects of their jobs to a high standard, they consistently emphasized the need to learn not only how to do specific things but also to learn how to learn. They believed that one of the reasons that they did well was because they were 'smart at getting smart'. The first rung has a very steep learning curve and you will earn recognition not only for how well you perform at each point in the learning curve but also for the speed with which you climb the curve. In this section, we cover how to climb the learning curve and get smart quickly.

> You will earn recognition not only for how well you perform at each point in the learning curve but also for the speed with which you climb the curve.

Put in the hours, particularly early on

Above all other advice this section has to offer is that, if you want to master the fundamentals of your job, you need to commit significant time. As we discussed in Chapter 1, commitment is a vital ingredient for success. One of the most important times to be committed is when you are in the 'ramp-up phase', as Mary Peters of Microsoft puts it. Mary explains that the ramp-up phase is the steepest part of the learning curve when you are faced with lots of new information to digest, unfamiliar tasks to perform and new people to work with. The ramp-up phase occurs in the early stages of any new task or project but is most severe in a new job.

Christy Roberts of Intuit recalls spending many hours at the office for the first few months. She came in early and stayed late – long after everyone else had left. She read materials to increase her knowledge and practised procedures such as beta-testing new software so that she learned how to be efficient, reliable and accurate. There was no element of so-called 'face time' here, only a real commitment to learning.

Chris Moritz of Teligent also made a personal commitment to master the field of telecommunications when he joined the company. He spent hours reading and speaking to people. He describes it as 'immersing' himself in his field. He read every tutorial he could find; he studied the vast nomenclature specific to the industry; and he learned the engineering principles behind telecom networks.

When Elizabeth Baker, formerly of Arthur Andersen, joined a small venture capital firm, she made it a habit for the first six months to read every single business case that entrepreneurs submitted to her firm, not just the ones assigned to her. She would read them in the evening at home or even at the weekend. She learned from those business cases that ultimately proved successful to recognize potentially successful companies, the essence of her business.

Take full advantage of training programmes

Many firms hold formal entry training programmes for their college and business school intakes.

A number of the executives interviewed went through training programmes as soon as they joined their companies. David Bruce of Aramark had a two-week programme where he learned all about Aramark's businesses. Rachel Lynn of Siebel Systems had a one-month training programme where she learned not just about Siebel Systems, but how to perform effectively in her job. Robert Styles of JP Morgan had a three-month training programme where he learned all about JP Morgan's business, the investment banking industry and how to handle specific aspects of his job. In my first job in investment banking, I had a four-month training programme that included several marked examinations on subjects ranging from accounting to securities law. My second job, as a management consultant, started off with a two-week training course.

In addition to the induction training, many firms offer ongoing structured training programmes that comprise intermittent courses lasting anywhere from a morning or afternoon to a couple of weeks. For Luis Costa of Procter & Gamble, the training was standardized; everyone took the same sets of courses. Mary Peters of Microsoft could request to go on specific courses if she could justify the time and expense. Jake Hammond of a major US management consulting company had a mix of standardized training and elective courses that he could take.

It may seem obvious to you that training programmes are useful tools for getting smart. However, many executives view training courses as a waste of time, and more of an excuse to have a break from 'real work' and to socialize with colleagues. Indeed, training programmes are often good fun; you make great friends and you experience a strong social environment. Apart from the mandatory training programmes, however, you will frequently find it difficult to find time and justification to attend specific training courses. However, the executives surveyed for this book strongly agree that you can get a lot from training programmes, but it is a matter of mindset. As Luis Costa of Procter & Gamble put it, 'You get out what you put in.'

John Abrahams of Credit Suisse First Boston had the opportunity to join the bank as a second-year analyst, having already performed highly for nearly a year at another

> You can get a lot from training programmes, but it is a matter of mindset... You get out what you put in.

bank. He explicitly chose to join as a first-year analyst to take advantage of the training programme offered to first-years. Such was the strength of his performance, which he in no small part attributes to the benefits of the training programme, that he ended up being promoted to associate early.

David Bruce of Aramark recognized the dual purpose of training programmes as an opportunity to network and make good friends, as well as to learn. He was diligent in class and made sure he learned the material presented but he also participated in social activities and made long-term friends and contacts, who continue to serve him well in his career. Strong and effective networks are a critical element for success on the first rung, and later in the book we discuss them in greater detail.

Rachel Lynn of Siebel Systems believes she was able to perform much better at her job because she paid close attention during her training courses – she asked lots of questions, took notes, thought hard about the direct application of the material she was learning, engaged the lecturers before and after class, stayed abreast of all the reading and completed her assignments to the best of her abilities.

Conduct basic research independently

Particularly where your job requires specific knowledge, you need to conduct basic research. If your job is focused on a specific market, you need to understand that market. If you are focused on a particular function, such as finance, you need to understand the principles of that function. In industries that are based on complex technologies or science, you need to understand at least the basic underpinnings of the technology or science behind the business.

The first challenge is to know what you need to research and the level of research required. Charlie Evans works for Chiron, a biotechnology firm. Charlie does not aspire to understand the detailed science behind genetic engineering and drug discovery, because he knows that scores of doctorate-trained scientists provide that level of expertise. Instead, he ensures he is familiar with the main elements of the research and development pathway, the requirements of clinical trials and the manufacturing process.

Chris Moritz of Teligent recognized the importance of understanding the technology behind the telecommunications business and made a personal commitment to developing a good understanding of it, although he also recognized that he was not there to develop the technology.

Luis Costa of Procter & Gamble worked in a job that was focused on a particular branded washing powder. He did not have to worry about all the other products in the Procter & Gamble portfolio. He knew that he needed to know the washing powder market inside out. In his first few weeks, he read report after report after report on the industry and developed a strong understanding of the market. He quickly learned that, in a marketing-oriented company like Procter & Gamble, he needed to understand the '4 Ps': product (what you sell), place (where you sell it), price (how much you sell it for) and promotion (how you market it to your target market). He made sure that he understood the 4 Ps of the washing powder market inside out by spending personal time reading up on the subject, for example by reading the bible of marketing, *Marketing Management* by Philip Kotler.

Take time to step back and understand the big picture

A number of executives felt that a broad understanding of the overall business of their organization was helpful to putting their role and business area in context.

Two frameworks that a few executives mentioned, which helped them understand the broad context of their business, come from Harvard Business School professor and famous author on competition and strategy Michael Porter (see *Competitive Strategy* and *Competitive Advantage*):

1. Porter's 'five forces' classify the influences that shape business markets. They are: barriers to entry (how difficult it is for new competitors to enter the market); competitors (how competitor behaviour shapes the market); customers (how customer power influences the market); substitutes (what alternative products or services affect or could affect the market); and suppliers (how supplier power influences the market).

2. Porter's value chain breaks the business model down into discrete units or functions. Consider a company like Ford that makes cars. It sources raw materials or parts, manufactures or builds them into cars and then sells the cars to customers. In its simplest form, Ford needs: a unit to handle supply of raw materials and parts to its factories and plants; a manufacturing unit to run the factories and plants; a unit to handle shipment of its cars to customer sales points; and a sales force to handle the selling. In reality, the business model is more complex, with many more units and layers of breakdown than described here, but a simplified value chain is a convenient tool for understanding the different areas of a business.

If you want to understand these frameworks more thoroughly, there is much material on them, and of course Porter's original books are a valuable resource. For now, understand that these frameworks are convenient tools to help you develop a big-picture appreciation of your job and company.

John Abrahams of Credit Suisse First Boston warns, however, that in time-critical situations you should focus on producing work to the highest standard and only when pressure has eased off should you spend time understanding the broader context for next time.

Develop and leverage a 'knowledge network'

Just as your colleagues are the best resource for finding information, they are also the best resource for getting smart. In any organization, most knowledge lies in the minds, on the desks or in the hard drives of executives around the organization. If you want to find out how the outbound logistics team manages shipments, you can probably find lots of theory on the subject and even some manuals, but the fastest way to learn is to speak to the people who know, just as the fastest way to collect information is to get it from the people who have access to it.

Just as Chris Moritz of Teligent relied on two engineers to get technical information when he needed it, so he leveraged them to help him learn about the technology and engineering aspects of telecommunication.

> Most knowledge lies in the minds, on the desks or in the hard drives of executives around the organization.

Mary Peters of Microsoft arranges meetings with firm experts to ask them questions and get up to speed on particular subjects. Christy Roberts of Intuit was required to beta-test a number of new software products to make sure that they worked well. When she first started her job, she did not wait to be assigned new software products to beta-test; she practised beta-testing on a number of software products that were assigned to more experienced beta-testers and sought their help in becoming expert. Her combination of proactiveness, enthusiasm for learning and willingness to ask colleagues for help meant that Christy became proficient without the pressure of having to get it right in a live situation.

> The people with the best insights on a particular activity are not necessarily the senior or intellectual office workers, but the people closest to the activity.

Dan Barker of US Robotics recognized the value of his colleagues to help him get smart quickly, but he also recognized that the people with the best insights on a particular activity are not necessarily the senior or intellectual office workers, but the people closest to the activity. For example, when he wanted to understand more about outbound logistics at US Robotics, Dan found that chatting to the fork-lift driver behind a pile of crates while he was lighting up on a cigarette break yielded great insights.

Mike Sandler of McMaster-Carr agrees. He has to work closely with a lot of blue-collar workers in a major distribution centre warehouse. When he wants to learn how a process in the warehouse could be improved or to understand how a particular thing works, he knows to ask the blue-collar workers first.

When building knowledge networks, it is important to be informal and to be respectful of people's time. Usually, people will be cooperative, but you should be attuned to the time when people are busy or under pressure. You should also keep interactions very focused and avoid wasting anyone's time.

In a nutshell – How to adopt a systematic approach

- Establish an efficient physical workspace.

- Methodically file physical documents.

- Methodically save and file electronic documents.

- Never go anywhere without an extra pen, notepad and calculator.

- Keep thorough notes.

- Make an early start.

- Plan ahead and use a diary.

- Begin and end your day with to-do lists.

- Learn to prioritize.

- Learn the short cuts.

- Do not procrastinate.

- Touch simple items only once.

- Put in the hours, particularly early on, to learn the fundamentals of your job.

- Take full advantage of training programmes.

- Conduct basic research independently.

- Take time to step back and understand the big picture.

- Develop and leverage a 'knowledge network'.

3

Develop into an excellent research analyst

Many of the high-flying executives researched for this book believe that their ability to excel at the core components of their job was important in differentiating them from their peers. As Elizabeth Baker of Arthur Andersen says: 'You must focus on producing good work.' For a first-runger, the core components of the job will almost certainly include researching information and performing analysis. Some first-runger jobs are inherently more analytical than others, but all first-runger jobs require, at the very least, a knowledge base that can only be built through research and exposure to large amounts of information.

Such is the learning curve in many new jobs in terms of sheer volume of information and knowledge that a significant proportion of the executives surveyed actually wished that they

> For a first-runger, the core components of the job will almost certainly include researching information and performing analysis.

had spent more time before they began their jobs learning about their industry and the knowledge required to perform in their role. Greater knowledge, they argued, would have made their initial job easier, provided them with a better understanding of their role and made them generally more productive.

Research and analytical skills are more intellectually demanding than organizational and time-management skills. However, even those jobs with a strong research and analysis orientation are actually not that difficult. While some executives highlight raw intelligence as a key factor in their first-rung success, they tend to view it more as a 'hygiene factor'; in other words, they believe that it is necessary to meet a certain threshold of intelligence to perform, but that, beyond the threshold, further intellectual firepower is not a great differentiator. When the managing director told the incoming class on the first day of my investment banking job that there were over 100 applicants for every position, the reality is that most of those applicants were probably intelligent and capable enough to do the functional aspects of the job to the minimum required standards. I have screened hundreds of CVs or résumés and interviewed many candidates for both investment banking and management consulting jobs, generally among the most selective in the marketplace. Rarely have I turned away candidates because I did not think they were intrinsically intelligent enough to handle the day-to-day tasks and projects the job entailed.

If not intelligence, what then is the key to you being a better research analyst than your peers? The answer is to make sure that you master the correct techniques and practices. This chapter will help you achieve greater mastery by providing you with advice on the correct techniques and the best practices. These have been specifically sourced from those executives whom I know to have been recognized as outstanding research analysts when they were first-rungers.

Producing insightful, rigorous and synthesized research

At the heart of every business is information. All major companies have highly sophisticated systems providing information such as comprehensive statistical data on shopping trends for supermarket companies or detailed clinical literature on drug trials for pharmaceutical companies. When you are on the first rung, one of your primary functions is to manage information and conduct research. Your bosses and colleagues will expect you to provide them with research that is relevant, succinct and timely. You must know what information to research and why, where to find it, how to access it and how to share it. To be an excellent information researcher you need to continue to build on your systematic approach to your work, as discussed in Chapter 2, by observing the principles set out in the following sections.

You must know what information to research and why, where to find it, how to access it and how to share it.

Clarify information requests

Whenever bosses ask you to provide some information, make sure you understand exactly what information they require and why. Too many first-rungers are afraid to ask for clarification for fear of appearing stupid. Sometimes, bosses may not think through their information request and only ask for some of the information they ultimately require. Alternatively, they may not articulate their request very clearly.

One way that executives mention to ensure that you know precisely what information bosses are seeking is to 'play back' the information request to them. This avoids forcing them to explain later when you return with the wrong or incomplete information. By articulating the information request in your own words, you allow bosses to correct any misunderstandings and even refine their original request.

Think for yourself

Providing bosses with the exact information requested is still not good enough. You must learn to think for yourself and provide everything that is needed to answer the question that underpins the information request. Not only will you make your bosses' jobs easier, but you will also gain greater understanding of your company's business and impress your bosses along the way. Adrian White of United Health Insurance found that most first-rungers are very capable at performing the superficial function of their job. They listen to their bosses' requests and do exactly what is asked of them, but they seek to understand only so far as to allow them to complete their task. He compares them to average students of calculus. In calculus, he explains, the average student memorizes formulae and applies them in standard calculus problems. However, when faced with unfamiliar problems, average students cannot apply memorized formulae and so fail to find solutions. Outstanding calculus students learn the underlying principles, why these principles apply and when to use them. They are able to handle both the familiar and the unfamiliar calculus problem.

When Mark Jackson of Dell started in his operations job, his boss assigned him eight or nine seemingly unrelated projects. By clarifying his boss's objectives, Mark learned that his boss was ultimately concerned with fixing some specific but poorly understood problems on the plant floor. He realized that what she really wanted was information to identify the true nature of the problems and to facilitate the finding of solutions. While remaining sensitive about not overstepping his bounds, Mark asked his boss if he could go and take a look at the plant floor. He proceeded to talk to plant-floor workers and even to his boss's peers to get the information required to solve the problem. Mark unearthed information that pointed to issues with bottlenecks and misaligned incentives across different groups of workers on the floor. As it turned out, Mark proved instrumental not just in identifying the problems but in solving them.

Build and leverage an 'information network'

The key to finding the right information is to know where information exists. All large firms have technology-based systems that centralize certain information. Often, you can access company library facilities, online proprietary internal search portals or external fee-based search portals on specific industry topics. Dotted throughout the company, you can find numerous databases, some formal and others created as part of specific projects. You need to find out where all these information sources or 'nodes' exist in your organization as soon as possible and learn how to access them and how much they cost if they are fee based. Get to know the people in the company library. Learn how to navigate the computer interface of relevant databases or, if access is limited, get to know those who do have access. Be prepared to spend extra time outside normal working hours getting up to speed; you will save more time in the long run.

Chris Moritz of Teligent learned that the way to excel at information gathering is to know the right people, as people are often the most useful 'information nodes'. He recalls having to collect information on the engineering aspects

> You need to find where all these information sources or 'nodes' exist in your organization as soon as possible.

of mobile telephony and found two engineers who were experts in this area to provide access. Every time he needed some information on the engineering side, he would rely on these two engineers.

Elizabeth Baker of Arthur Andersen is also a big believer in leveraging her colleagues when she is looking for information. If she does not know whom to call on, it is likely that one of her colleagues will either know directly or know someone who knows.

Both Chris and Elizabeth built and used 'information networks' to great effect. We talk more about networks later in the book but, for now, know that your co-workers are the greatest resource you have available to you.

Become an information node

Paul Graham of Wasserstein Perella & Co also recognizes that there are certain people who are 'nodes' of information in a firm – people who seem to have access to all the information on a particular topic or in a particular area. Paul went one step further than building an 'information network': he became an important node in it. For everything he worked on, he made sure he had all the information to hand on his desk. He was meticulous in storing and filing, and quickly developed the reputation for being the first person to approach when looking for information. As he puts it: 'Become the "go-to" person for any information to do with anything you have worked on.'

> Become the 'go-to' person for any information to do with anything you have worked on.

Don't forget the internet

You should always try to use company or company-recognized third-party sources of information whenever possible. You can trust the reliability and accuracy of the information if it comes from a recognizable and widely used source. However, sometimes you cannot find everything you need through the standard corporate channels. The internet should be your backstop. As John Abrahams of Credit Suisse First Boston puts it: 'There really is no excuse for not being able to come up with some information on any topic. The internet has everything.'

Jake Hammond had to cold-call several executives for one of his recent projects at a major consulting firm. He had no names, only a requirement that the individuals must be senior and work in a specific area of their company. One trick he used to great effect was to look up conferences on the internet in the relevant area – he knew that conferences often list the titles and companies of the main speakers. With the names, titles and companies he extracted from the conference websites, he was able to use the company switchboard to put him through to the cold-call individuals.

Source and date your information for rigour

Information is as valid as its source. Whenever you provide any information, you must always cite the source and, particularly if it is related to current events, the date the information was generated. Often, I have seen first-rungers state a fact confidently, only to lose their poise completely on being unable to provide a source when probed. In written documents, cite all sources in footnotes or write them directly in the text.

Summarize, synthesize and use the one-pager to highlight insights

Just as you should think for yourself and provide your bosses with information that helps them achieve their objectives instead of just providing the information they request, so you should summarize and synthesize information to help them focus on the most important elements. When Elizabeth Baker of Arthur Andersen digs up some information to share with her colleagues and bosses, she routinely reads through it first and provides a one-page memo summarizing the main elements and synthesizing any important insights that arise from the report.

In fact, many executives extol the merits of limiting all kinds of briefing notes and summaries to the 'one-pager'. The 'one-pager'

> Many executives extol the merits of limiting all kinds of briefing notes and summaries to the 'one-pager'.

is not easy to prepare because it requires you to recognize the most important points and synthesize them with crisp language.

Some executives noted that another way to help your boss digest a significant volume of information is to highlight the key pieces of information. For example, if you have produced a press search on some topic for the last two years, you might find hundreds of relevant articles. While your boss may have asked you for the full press search, highlight those particular articles that are the most informative and let your boss know that, if he or she reads nothing else, these should be read. Your boss will appreciate your proactive prioritization and initiative.

Performing rock-solid analysis

If there is analysis to be done, first-rungers are usually the ones who have to do it. Your education should have taught you the basic quantitative methods and mathematics required to perform in most first-rung jobs. It is worth noting one big difference between your schooling and your work, however – you receive no partial credit in your job. In the workplace, you have to get the answer right and, where the answer is contingent on assumptions and methodology, you need to be technically correct in your approach. The purpose of analysis in the workplace is to provide insights to aid decision making that often have significant financial ramifications. This is why your analysis has to be flawless; one seemingly harmless mistake can cost your company a very large sum of money. Developing your analytical skills and making sure that your analysis is rock-solid, however, require not just a good foundation in quantitative methods but also a strong understanding of how to use spreadsheets.

> Your analysis has to be flawless; one seemingly harmless mistake can cost your company a very large sum of money.

For the purposes of this book, it is inappropriate to go to the level of detail required to understand fully most of the necessary quantitative methods and the inner workings of spreadsheets. There are far better resources available, and any trip to the computer section of a bookshop will also reveal a large number of very thick books on how to use spreadsheets. Where these books fail, and where this book can help, is in providing a sense of priority; this book tells you the most important things you need to know for most first-rung roles and synthesizes these essentials. In the following pages, I cover the most important quantitative methods, the key lessons, functions and tools for effective spreadsheet analysis and general principles for rock-solid analysis.

To get the most out of the remainder of this chapter and to master rock-solid analysis, I suggest the following approach:

1. Read through the material once to get an overview of the knowledge and skills that you require to perform rock-solid analysis. Take your time, as this material is the densest in the book.
2. If you are new to spreadsheets, go and buy a tutorial book and use it to get comfortable with the basics and to learn more about the more complex analytical tools described below.
3. Refer back to this chapter whenever you have analysis to perform to ensure you are:
   – using the right analytical tools for the kind of analysis you are performing;
   – following the principles to produce rock-solid analysis.
4. Learn how to do compound average growth rates (CAGRs) and weighted averages immediately.

Some of you will already have a strong grasp of quantitative methods and spreadsheets, particularly if you have majored in or read scientific or quantitative subjects as an undergraduate. If you fall into such a group, you may want to skip much of this chapter, although I would still strongly recommend that you spend time reading through the sections entitled 'The first-runger core toolkit for advanced analytics' and 'Overall principles for rock-solid analysis', as well as the section in Appendix I entitled 'Key elements of spreadsheet functionality for formatting'.

The essential quantitative methods

This section provides descriptions of the most important quantitative methods, mathematics and statistics that first-rungers need to be able to apply effortlessly in most roles. For two methods, calculating CAGRs and using weighted averages, I go into detailed methodology, but for most I provide overviews. Do not be worried if you do not know all of these quantitative methods as you begin your job; they are relatively easy to learn.

The following, then, are the key elements of quantitative analysis that you should feel comfortable handling.

Basic arithmetic and percentages

Addition, subtraction, multiplication and division are universally required and you should ensure that you have a reasonably sharp mental capability to perform basic arithmetic without resorting to a calculator. Percentages are important for understanding relative measures, drawing comparisons and describing growth rates. For example, if you want to compare how effective two companies are at converting their revenues into profits, you need to use percentages, as one company may have much larger revenues than the other.

Compound average growth rates

CAGRs (in mathematics, they are also called 'geometric means') are important for understanding the average growth rate over a time series and for being able to draw comparisons against other data. For example, suppose you want to compare the economic performance of the United States and France over the last 50 years. You might look at gross domestic product (GDP) and find GDP growth data year on year for the last 50 years. You might find that in some years the United States has higher year-on-year GDP figures and in other years France has higher GDP figures. You might be able to 'eyeball' the data and see that the United States has more consistently had higher year-on-year GDP growth than France, but the only real way to contrast the performance of the two countries over the entire period is by looking at the CAGRs. Many first-rungers find CAGRs difficult; I recall a number of my peers struggling to calculate them, and I still see mid-level executives struggling too. However, they are not so hard to calculate, and it is one of the two quantitative methods whose calculation we will run through. Calculate CAGRs by:

■ dividing the last number by the first number in a series to get the total growth over the time period;
■ then applying a 'power' equal to the inverse of the number of time intervals; and finally
■ subtracting 1 and multiplying by 100 to convert to a percentage.

For example, consider the following series of annual profit numbers in millions of pounds: 5, 10, 13, 21, 45 and 56:

- The total growth over the entire series is 56/5, which equals 11.2 times (1,120 per cent).
- The number of time intervals is 5 (note, this is not the number of numbers, but is one less than the number of numbers) and therefore the inverse of the number of time periods is 1/5 or 0.2.
- Apply the power of 0.2 to 11.2 to give 1.621.
- Finally, subtract 1 and multiply by 100, and you have a CAGR of 62.1 per cent.

In other words, in order for a company with profit of £5 million in year one to reach a profit of £56 million in year six, it has to grow its profit at an annual growth rate of 62.1 per cent.

Weighted averages

In addition to three types of unweighted averages (mean, median and mode) that we discuss in the next section on statistics and probability, you also need to understand weighted averages and when to apply them. Weighted averages are the second of the two quantitative methods that we will run through. Look at the data in Table 3.1, which shows the five-year historical CAGR in total sales for five companies. Suppose that these companies are the main companies in a certain industry, and you want to calculate the five-year historical sales CAGR for that industry. You might take the average of the sales growth of each of these companies as a proxy for the industry. Assuming you are using the arithmetic mean (see below) for the average, you would sum up the CAGRs and divide by 5, the number of companies, to get the answer of 22.2 per cent.

Table 3.1 *Mean five-year CAGR*

Company	Sales (£m)	Five-year CAGR
1	100	5%
2	150	10%
3	450	45%
4	75	37%
5	200	14%
		Average (mean) = 22.2%

This answer, however, is the unweighted average. In other words, you have ignored the fact that some companies have significantly more sales than other companies; for example, company 3 has £450 million in sales, while company 4 has only £75 million. Table 3.2 proves that this approach calculates an unweighted (or equal-weighted) average. Weighting each company's sales figure equally at 20 per cent, multiplying it by each company's respective CAGR and summing the resultant unweighted contributions to the average yields exactly the same result as the arithmetic mean calculation.

Table 3.2 *Unweighted contributions to the average*

Five-year CAGR	Weight	Unweighted contribution
5%	20%	1.0%
10%	20%	2.0%
45%	20%	9.0%
37%	20%	7.4%
14%	20%	2.8%
	100%	
		Unweighted average = 22.2%

Instead of applying even weights to each company's sales figure, you should apply weightings proportional to the sales per company relative to the sum of sales of all the companies. Table 3.3 shows this result.

Table 3.3 *Weighted contributions to the average*

Company	Sales (£m)	Five-year CAGR	Weight	Weighted contribution
1	100	5%	10.3%	0.51%
2	150	10%	15.4%	1.54%
3	450	45%	46.2%	20.77%
4	75	37%	7.7%	2.85%
5	200	14%	20.5%	2.87%
			100.0%	
				Weighted average = 28.54%

You can see that the weight for company 1 is equal to its sales (£100 million) divided by the sum of sales for all five companies (£975 million), which equals 10.3 per cent. The weighted contribution (to the weighted average) is this weight of 10.3 per cent times the five-year CAGR for company 1 (5 per cent) and equals 0.51 per cent. The sum of the weighted contributions of each company equals the weighted average of 28.54 per cent, a very different result from the unweighted average.

Basic statistics and probability

A lot of decision making in business is based on statistical analysis because a lot of business has to deal with large numbers, for example customer data or flows

A lot of decision making in business is based on statistical analysis because a lot of business has to deal with large numbers.

of product components through a manufacturing process. Statistics and probability can get very technical, and there are lots of complex methods that you do not need to worry about unless you have a highly specialized role. However, you should at least have an understanding of the following methods and be able to apply them in your analysis.

The mean, median and mode

There are three types of unweighted arithmetic averages: the mean, the median and the mode:

- The mean is the sum of a series of numbers divided by the number of numbers in the series.
- The median is the middle number in a series or the number that 50 per cent of the numbers in the series are higher than and 50 per cent are lower than.
- The mode is the most frequent number in the series.

They are rarely the same, and understanding the differences is important because the point of the average is to illustrate a 'representative' value for a sample or population (this is why the sample must also be representative of the larger population). If a series of numbers has many outliers on the high end of the series, the mean will be biased towards these outliers, and the median is probably a better indicator of a representative value.

For example, suppose you are working in a distribution centre for a computer company and have to manage the shipment of computers to customers' homes. Suppose further that, for every 100 computers that you ship out, 90 get to customers' homes in three days, but, because of some problems in the distribution centre, 10 computers take 30 days to deliver. What is the representative delivery time that your customers might expect? If you use the mean, the answer is 5.7 days, while the median and mode would both give you an answer of three days. Think this is playing with numbers? Not so. Suppose that your main competitor manages to ship computers to all of its customers in four days without any variation. If you were simply basing your decision on the mean delivery time of 5.7 days, you might decide to overhaul the entire distribution system to reduce the time across all orders to outperform your competitor. If you were to look at both the mean and the median, you would immediately recognize that, when the system works, as it does for 90 per cent of customers, you are better than your competitor, and so you would focus your management attention on the 10 per cent where distribution goes very wrong.

Standard deviation

While the mean, median and mode describe a representative value, standard deviation describes variation around a representative value. It is not a straightforward formula, and you do not ordinarily need to know how to calculate it from first principles. You do need to know what information it conveys, and you should be able to calculate it using spreadsheets.

Why is it important? Recall the example above of the computer distribution centre used to highlight the importance of understanding the differences between the mean, the median and the mode as representative values. In that example, we saw that, by understanding these differences, in particular between the mean and the median, it was possible to understand something about the variation in the shipment times across the customer base that proved important when it came to making improvements in the distribution centre. However, the mean, median and mode provide only limited information on the type of variation, and sometimes, as we shall see when we discuss normal distributions, the mean, median and mode are identical even when there is wide variation in a sample. When they are identical, they tell you nothing about variation. Standard deviation, however, explicitly describes the degree of variation and therefore further supports critical decision making on issues involving large numbers.

Standard deviation is denoted by the symbol sigma (σ), and there are some rules of thumb that you need to know about sigma. In a normal distribution, all values in a population that lie within one standard deviation, or one sigma of the mean, represent two-thirds of the population; all values that lie within two sigma represent 95 per cent of the population; and all values that lie within three sigma represent 99 per cent of the population. These rules of thumbs will help you quickly assess variation and make intelligent observations without the need for performing detailed analysis.

Let me provide an example. Suppose you are working in a call centre that deals with customer queries. Your job is to help ensure that customer experience is positive, for example not having to wait for a long time to get through to a customer representative. Now suppose that your boss asks you how long the average customer waits before a customer representative picks up the phone, and you provide an answer based on the mean of all the data that the average customer waits 30 seconds. That sounds like a reasonably short wait, and you might think that there is no problem. Suppose, however, that within one sigma the range is five seconds to five minutes. You can quickly mentally calculate that 16 to 17 people out of every 100 have to wait over five minutes (one-third of, or 33 out of every 100, customers are outside one sigma, half of which, 16 to 17, wait longer than five minutes and half of which, the other 16 to 17, wait less than five seconds). You are now in a position to recommend the need for improvement in managing call wait times and improvement in the overall customer experience where less sophisticated analysts might have fallen short.

Statistical distributions, particularly normal and skewed distributions

In our discussions above on the mean, median and mode and the standard deviation, you saw how they are all important in the making of business decisions that involve large numbers, whether those are about managing delivery times of home computer shipments or customer wait times in a call centre. Ultimately, to make the most robust decisions that involve large numbers you need to understand distributions. In fact, the mean, mode, median and the standard deviation collectively provide information on the shape of the distribution and, while they provide useful information on their own, only through understanding the full nature of distributions can you make truly robust decisions. For example, suppose you work for a clothing manufacturer that is trying to decide, for every 100 pieces of clothes it makes, how many should be extra large, how many should be large, how many should be medium etc. One way to arrive at the answer is by looking at distributions of the size of people in the general population.

If you were to look at the size of people in the general population, you would naturally expect to see a range. If you were to plot the size of everyone in a population on a graph, however, you would find that it forms a symmetrical bell-shaped curve, as shown in Figure 3.1. The highest point of the curve is the most frequently observed size in the population (the mode) and it is typically in the centre of the range of values because there are roughly as many people larger than this height as there are smaller (the median), the fact that the distribution is symmetrical also makes this number the mean.

The clothing manufacturer could use this bell-shaped curve to figure out the proportions of each size. It would produce most of the medium sizes to fit those around the mean, because this covers the largest part of the population; then it would produce fewer large and small sizes and even fewer extra large and extra small sizes. Furthermore, because the bell-shaped curve is symmetrical, it would produce an equal number of

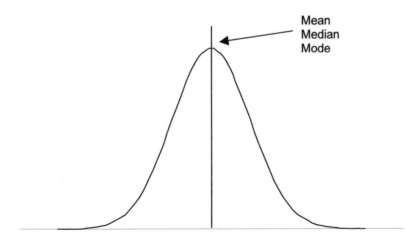

Mean
Median
Mode

Figure 3.1 *The normal distribution*

large to small and an equal number of extra large to extra small sizes. The precise numbers per hundred would depend on the specific numbers that generate the bell-shaped curve. This bell-shaped curve is also called the 'normal distribution' and is so called because it is the most common distribution pattern observed in statistics (it is also called the 'Gaussian distribution' after the mathematician Karl Friedrich Gauss). In fact, if you know that a set of numbers is normally distributed, you can use the mean and the standard deviation to perform this kind of analysis very quickly.

However, not all distributions are normal. The skewed distribution is one where the population of values is not symmetrically distributed; in other words, one side of the bell-shaped curve is fatter or longer than the other, as shown in the positively skewed distribution in Figure 3.2.

If the skewed distribution in Figure 3.2 had represented the sizes in the population, the clothing manufacturer would have to have produced a very different mix of sizes with many more large and extra large clothes than small and extra small clothes. The reason why skewed distributions are important to understand is because many business assumptions assume normal distributions erroneously. Many companies have made horrendous mistakes because they did not appreciate the 'skewness' in critical data sets such as customer distributions.

The skewed distribution produces different values for the mean, the mode and the median because it is asymmetrical. For example, in the

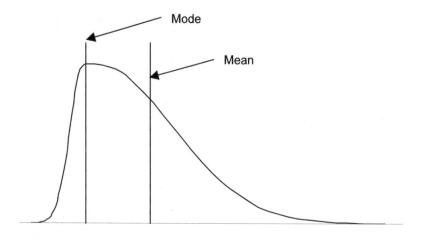

Figure 3.2 *A positively skewed distribution*

positively skewed distribution in Figure 3.2, the mean is greater than the mode (and the median), while in negatively skewed distributions it is less.

Correlation

The ability to find relationships within data sets is a critical requirement in the first-rung analytic toolkit. Drawing relationships in data begins with measuring correlations.

Correlations are easy to understand on an intuitive level. Imagine that you are going to open an umbrella shop and you want to work out where you should open your shop to get the most sales. Intuitively you would probably look at two things. The first thing you might look at is where it rains the most, and the second thing you might consider is where there are the most people. You might conclude, therefore, that an urban location with high levels of rainfall would make most sense. In other words, rainfall and population density are correlated with umbrella sales. Unfortunately, lots of relationships are not so intuitively correlated as in this umbrella example, and sometimes correlations may even be extremely counter-intuitive. The only way to assess correlation is quantitatively.

What do you need to know from a quantitative methods point of view? Understanding correlation between two variables requires understanding of how one variable changes with respect to the other variable. In other words, you need to understand the mathematical relationship between the two variables. From your school mathematics, you may recall that there are many different formulae that describe how the variable y changes with respect to x, for example you probably came across linear, logarithmic, exponential and parabolic relationships.

The good news is that you do not need to worry about all these different formulae. The one quantitative method to check for relationships in a large set of data that you do need to know is the 'linear regression', which looks for a linear relationship. A linear regression produces two outputs: the linear formula describing the relationship between the two variables (this will take the form of $y = mx + b$ for variables x and y); and something called the 'correlation coefficient'

> The good news is that you do not need to worry about all these different formulae. The one quantitative method to check for relationships in a large set of data that you do need to know is the 'linear regression'.

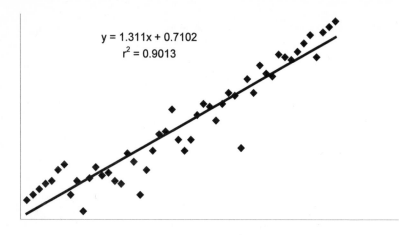

$$y = 1.311x + 0.7102$$
$$r^2 = 0.9013$$

Figure 3.3 *A linear regression*

or 'r^2'. If you do a linear regression graphically in a spreadsheet, the program will try to find the 'best-fit' line for the data, based on the linear formula. Figure 3.3 is a scatter plot where each point is generated by a value for each of two variables. You can see the best-fit line and you can see the formula that describes the line where m = 1.311 and b = 0.7102.

The most important piece of information in a linear regression is not the formula, but the r^2, which is a measure of the robustness of the correlation relationship, more commonly known as 'significance'. A more significant relationship has a higher r^2 and essentially tells you that the relationship is unlikely to exist through chance. The reason that the r^2 is more important than the formula is because knowing that a relationship exists is usually all that managers need to know in order to make a decision. The main value in the formula is in indicating whether the correlation is positive or negative – whether the value of one variable increases (positive) or decreases (negative) with respect to increases in the other variable. In other words, does the line slope upwards or downwards? How much it slopes up or down and where it intercepts, as defined by the formula, are usually relatively unimportant.

The basics of spreadsheets

Before you can leverage the computational power of spreadsheets and be a master of rock-solid analysis, you need to understand some of the basics of how they work. Appendix I covers three areas of spreadsheet basics:

- **key elements of spreadsheet functionality for analysis** – provides a brief overview of core spreadsheet concepts that you will need to understand to perform any kind of analysis;
- **key elements of spreadsheet functionality for formatting** – provides a brief overview of what you need to know to make spreadsheets user-friendly on-screen and through print;
- **the 10 most commonly used mathematics and statistics spreadsheet functions** – lists the basic functions that will form the core of all basic analysis.

Three important functions to help build spreadsheet models

To build more complex models and run more sophisticated analysis, you should know how to use the following three functions:

- **IF.** Allows you to define one of two results depending on the conditions of the cells to which the formula is linked. The IF function can also be 'nested' (IF formulae built within IF formulae) and/or used with other logical functions such as AND to determine very precise conditions for a particular calculation. Suppose you are looking at a set of data for a superstore that offers customers a 10 per cent discount on order sizes over £100 of goods. Now suppose you have a data set of customer data and their order sizes organized in columns and you need to calculate how much to charge each customer. You could use an IF function, which might look like the following (where 'ORDER SIZE' represents the relative cell reference that contains the data for the relevant customer): IF('ORDER SIZE'<100,'ORDER SIZE','ORDER SIZE'*0.9). This formula automatically detects those orders worth £100 or more and produces the chargeable value after applying a

10 per cent discount to the order size. For order sizes below £100, it would produce the same value as the order size.

■ **SUMIF.** SUMIF calculates the sum of only certain entries that meet certain criteria in a series of data, for example numbers above a certain threshold. Suppose that you wanted to calculate the proportion of the total value of all orders that qualify for a discount compared to those that do not qualify, in the same example as used above. You might use SUMIF to sum all those orders worth £100 and above, and again use SUMIF to sum all those orders worth less than £100. You could then quickly calculate the proportion to each other or each proportion to the total value of all orders. Another similar function is COUNTIF, which follows the same process with a series of data but performs a different operation – counting certain entries rather than summing them. You might, for example, use this function to calculate the proportion of orders, as opposed to total order value, that qualify for a discount compared to those that do not qualify.

■ **VLOOKUP.** This searches for a cell entry in an array of data by relating the cell entry positionally to a 'field marker'. This can be very useful if you are consolidating data from multiple sources. Suppose that you are a company that sells multiple products to its customers, and you want to understand the product mix of your customer base. You might find that each product has its own set of data in different spreadsheets, and you need to consolidate the data into one spreadsheet in order to analyse product mix. The way you might approach this problem is to create a new spreadsheet with a full list of customers (the field markers) in one column and label additional columns to capture volume data (how much customers have spent on a particular product) by product. You could then set up a VLOOKUP formula for each product that searches through source data for each particular customer and returns the value of the adjacent entry for product volumes. Extrapolating these VLOOKUP formulae across all the customers (using 'drag and drop', for example) will provide you with the data set you need to perform analysis on product mix. One note: syntax is important in VLOOKUP – in this example, it is likely that not every source data set will spell its customer names identically, so you will probably have to 'clean the data' and ensure consistent syntax in all source data before being able to use VLOOKUP properly.

The first-runger core toolkit for advanced analytics

The power of spreadsheets comes to the fore with 10 powerful tools that can do in a few moments what would literally take days of work to do longhand. These functions are absolute lifesavers, as they are easy to perform and allow you to organize data systematically and find important relationships, trends and messages quickly, and thereby show great mastery of the data. Again, this section will not tell you how actually to run the following functions. It is meant to provide you with insight on which tool is most appropriate for different types of advanced analysis:

> These functions are absolute life-savers, as they are easy to perform and allow you to organize data systematically and find important relationships, trends and messages quickly.

1. **Pivot tables.** Personally, I think pivot tables are the coolest of tools in spreadsheets – to the extent that anything about spreadsheets could be considered cool, that is. Imagine that you have a massive array of customer data for a supermarket store, including the personal details of tens of thousands of customers (nationality, address, age and occupation) and that for each customer you have 10 different product categories, ranging from fruit and vegetables to domestic cleaning products, and details of each customer's total spend by product category over the last year. If you had to produce analysis that shows the split of total spend by category by customer occupation, how would you do it? There are actually a few ways to approach the problem, but by far the simplest way is to produce a pivot table. It will take you 30 seconds to set up the pivot table, and the result is almost instantaneous. What is even cooler about a pivot table is that once you have set up one pivot table on an array of data you can cut the data any way you want within the same table. You can also break down each axis to various levels of granularity and in various orders. For example, on one axis you might have all customers grouped by nationality and then, within each nationality, their occupation and, within their occupation, their age; alternatively, you could have age first, then nationality and then occupation. You can also use a different operator for the table output, such as count, sum, average etc.

2. **Data tables.** Data tables are great for performing sensitivity, scenario or 'what-if' analysis. Sensitivity analysis is an important part of modelling, because it provides insights into how an output varies with changes to critical inputs or 'drivers'. For example, a financial valuation model of a business is heavily driven by the growth rate (the CAGR) of the business and by the discount rate. Using a data table you can see the set of different outputs with different inputs. You can construct single- or dual-variable data tables. Single-variable data tables show how output varies against one variable, either the growth rate or the discount rate in our example. Dual-variable tables show how output varies against both variables simultaneously. In other words, the table will display data, varying different inputs for growth rate against different inputs for discount rates.

3. **Scenarios.** Scenarios are similar to data tables in that they allow you to vary inputs and see the change in output. However, unlike data tables, scenarios can vary more than two inputs. Most models have a number of inputs and assumptions that drive output. Scenarios allow you to 'pre-programme' sets of inputs. Typically most models include a base case, a conservative case and an aggressive case. By programming these scenarios, you can quickly change cases and do not have to record separately the set of inputs composing each case and then change each input individually.

4. **Goalseek.** Goalseek is also a useful tool for 'what-if' analysis. Unlike data tables or scenarios that vary outputs by changing inputs, goalseek allows you to set your output and see what a particular input needs to be to result in that output. In a financial valuation model, for example, you might want to see what the growth rate would have to be for a business to be worth £100 million. Goalseek would allow you to find that input.

5. **Solver.** Solver is similar to goalseek in that it also allows you to set your output to drive your inputs. However, it is more powerful than goalseek in that it allows you to set your output by changing more than one input at a time. Like goalseek and data tables, solver is a useful tool to perform 'what-if' analysis.

6. **Sort.** Sort is a simple function that allows you to organize data in an array, for example to recall the customer database for a supermarket store. You might want the data organized from top to bottom by

occupation, then by nationality and then by age. Sort will organize the data in this way.

7. **Subtotal.** Subtotal is always used with 'sort', as it requires data to be organized in some logical sequence to work. Subtotals allow you to do similar analysis to data tables but with far greater restrictions. For example, suppose you wanted to see the average age of your customer base by nationality. Subtotal would allow you to do this very quickly.

8. **Grouping (and ungrouping).** If you ever use the subtotal tool, you will notice that you can view the data at different orders of granularity. For example, you could see the data set with the age for every customer, just the average age by nationality or just the average age for the overall customer base. Subtotal automatically groups data into these levels of granularity. Grouping allows you to achieve the same result with any data. By grouping a set of rows or columns, you can organize views of different levels of granularity for your own data. Ungrouping, of course, undoes this effect.

9. **Autofilter.** Autofilter is also useful for refining views of large data sets. For example, if you wanted to see only entries for customers from one geographical area who buy household products, autofilter would be the best tool.

10. **Audit.** The audit tools allow you to trace the linkages in cell formulae. It is particularly useful when trying to understand how an existing spreadsheet is put together and also for debugging.

Overall principles for rock-solid analysis

Use primary sources for greatest accuracy

Information underpins analysis. Just as reliable sources validate the accuracy and reliability of information, so reliable sources are important for good analysis. The best sources are primary. A company annual report is an example of a primary source, while an industry report that aggregates its data from annual reports is a secondary source. Primary sources are more accurate and reliable than derivative sources because they are the origin of the information. Just as in the children's game 'Telephone call', mistakes increasingly crop up when information is passed further from its origin. When one of the interviewed executives compiles quarterly financial reports, he uses the direct output of management account systems; he does not rely on any secondary sources such as reports that have come from other executives.

Other executives note, however, that using primary sources is often more time-consuming than using secondary or tertiary sources, because secondary and tertiary sources often combine the information you need in one place. For example, when you need to analyse several companies, although the relevant information exists in each company's annual report, save time by using a secondary-source industry report that aggregates most of the numbers in one place.

You need to recognize the trade-off between accuracy and time here and make a judgement call. Lean towards accuracy and primary sources when the analysis is critically important and opt for time efficiency and secondary sources when time pressure is the greater consideration.

Validate assumptions

Often analysis requires more than factual inputs. You need to make assumptions. Any analysis, for example, that includes forecasting by definition includes assumptions of the future. While you can ensure that you use correct and appropriate factual inputs by using primary sources, you need to exercise judgement when making assumptions. There is an expression in financial modelling, 'junk in, junk out', which means that, no matter how good your analytic methods are, if the assumptions and inputs are wrong then the answer is wrong.

> There is an expression in financial modelling, 'junk in, junk out', which means that, no matter how good your analytic methods are, if the assumptions and inputs are wrong then the answer is wrong.

As a first-runger, you have to rely on limited experience when exercising your judgement, which makes it hard to make appropriate assumptions. You must validate your assumptions by testing them with others. Often you can rely on immediate colleagues if your analysis is generic. In cases where you require specific expert validation, you need to find out who the experts are. Carl Moran of General Electric asked his boss where to find experts to help him perform some operational pivot-table analysis in his business area and approached them to test, validate and refine his assumptions.

Kirk Williams of Chrysler recalls analysing the projected figures for a new van. Much of the analysis Kirk had to perform was benchmarking the figures for other vehicles. In this case, he recalls spending several meetings with experts, going through every line item in his model, checking each assumption. One expert would tell him that he needed to use a different benchmark (a benchmark is a reference number based on precedent or similar instances, typically in other companies) for one part, and another would tell him that the cost of a component was $8 million, not $5 million, for the expected production run. When Kirk presented his analysis, he cited these experts, lending his analysis enormous credibility.

Organize your analysis

The best first-rungers perform clear and easy-to-follow analysis (they continue to adopt a systematic approach even in the organization of their end-products). A standard followed by a number of investment banking first-rungers is to use a minimum of four spreadsheets for anything other than the most basic analysis. The first sheet provides an introduction that explains the purpose of the analysis and provides any other relevant information. The second sheet contains all inputs and assumptions and also includes sources, dates and notes explaining the rationale behind assumptions. The third sheet contains all the formulae and calculations that underpin the analysis, and the fourth sheet contains the outputs from the third page in an easy-to-read format.

You do not have to follow the same organizational structure as above, although it is a good one, but you should ensure that your work is highly organized and structured in some fashion. The best litmus test is whether someone who has not seen the analysis before can follow it.

> The best litmus test is whether someone who has not seen the analysis before can follow it.

Always fully link calculated numbers

If you have organized your spreadsheet well, with all your inputs on one page and all the calculations on another sheet, your calculations should automatically be linked to inputs or the outputs of other calculations. However, it is easy to be lazy and start typing numbers directly into the formulae of calculations. Do not make this mistake; you will lose flexibility in your analysis, and make it harder to check and debug if it is complex. Should your boss wish you to rerun your analysis with different assumptions or with new information, instead of changing only the input sheet you will have to audit the entire calculation sheet to be sure that your calculations reflect the changed inputs.

Never hard-wire numbers

If there is one cast-iron rule to follow it is: never hard-wire numbers in a spreadsheet. The only hard-wire numbers should be direct inputs. All other num-

> If there is one cast-iron rule to follow it is: never hard-wire numbers in a spreadsheet.

bers should be calculated. Hard-wiring numbers is even worse than not fully linking calculations, because it replaces a formula or a direct link to a formula with a number that remains fixed regardless of changes to inputs. On several occasions I have inherited analysis from another first-runger and needed to update the spreadsheets with new numbers. More than a few times, after checking the inputs and auditing the full set of calculated cells, I have discovered that one of the outputs was hard-wired. Someone had typed in a number that had presumably been calculated on paper or with a calculator. Had I not spotted this mistake, the analysis would have been wrong. It is likely that the first-runger at fault had updated the spreadsheet and had forgotten about the hard-wired number.

Use multiple short formulae instead of long single formulae

While you will not get partial credit for less-than-perfect analysis, one principle you should continue to follow from your school maths classes is to show your workings. Look at this formula used to calculate a corporate discount rate in discounted cash flow valuation models:

$$r_c = ((r_f + (\beta*(r_m - r_f)))*E/V) + ((r_d*(1 - t_c))*D/V)$$

where:

r_c = corporate discount rate
r_d = corporate debt rate
r_f = risk-free rate
r_m = stock market return rate
t_c = corporate tax rate
E = value of equity
D = value of debt
V = total value of corporate (equity + debt)
ß = covariance of corporate stock price with stock market

This is a complex-looking formula, and you should not be worried if it looks like gobbledegook to you. The point to note is how you input this formula into a spreadsheet. You could type all the relevant data into one calculation and produce the answer in one step. Best practice, however, is to break up this formula into discrete sub-formulae, and combine them into a 'master formula'. This way, you are less likely to make mistakes in the calculation, and if you do make mistakes you can spot them much more easily. Furthermore, your colleagues will find it much easier to audit spreadsheets that avoid long individual calculations.

For example, I would probably break this formula down into four sub-formulae:

r_c = (sub-formula 1*sub-formula 2) + (sub-formula 3* sub-formula 4)

where:

sub-formula 1 = $(r_f + (ß*(r_m - r_f)))$
sub-formula 2 = E/V
sub-formula 3 = $(r_d*(1 - t_c))$
sub-formula 4 = D/V

Triangulate

Rarely is there only one way to do a piece of analysis. Usually, there are many approaches. Alternative approaches can even rely on completely different data and assumptions. A useful way to gain

> A useful way to gain confidence that a complex piece of analysis is reliable and accurate is to test some of the key outputs by applying other analytical techniques.

confidence that a complex piece of analysis is reliable and accurate is to test some of the key outputs by applying other analytical techniques. In the example above, you can also calculate the discount rate by analysing the price to earnings ratio (P/E) and the earnings growth rate. In fact, the full output of a valuation exercise using a discount rate, the value, can be compared against a value implied by a P/E ratio.

Triangulation does not mean that you have to spend triple the time on complex analysis. George Malone of Goldman Sachs employed 'back-of-the-envelope' calculations to triangulate. These are 'quick and dirty' calculations that are not refined but provide ballpark figures that allow you to double-check outputs. When John Abrahams of Credit Suisse First Boston used to perform full valuations using a discounted cash flow model, employing a discount rate like the one shown above to reduce all expected future cash flows to a single present value, he knew that such models are notoriously sensitive to inputs and that even slight adjustments to sales growth rates, the discount rate or the profit margin can have a major impact on value. To triangulate, he would find a similar company in the market and look at its price to earnings ratio, and then multiply that ratio to the current earnings of the company he was trying to value to imply its current price. The cash flow model would take days, even weeks, to get right, but he could do his back-of-the-envelope calculation in 30 seconds to make sure that he was coming up with a sensible value.

Sanity-check your answers

The danger of getting into deep analysis is that then you 'cannot see the wood for the trees'. By focusing so much on the analytic techniques and the organization

> By focusing so much on the analytic techniques and the organization of the spreadsheet, you can easily miss what can only be described as stupid mistakes.

of the spreadsheet, you can easily miss what can only be described as stupid mistakes. Let me provide a (somewhat extreme) example of a surprisingly common mistake. Suppose you are performing a very simple piece of analysis such as forecasting sales five years from now. For argument's sake, let us say that you work for a mature retail business. You might reasonably expect that your business's overall growth rate will be in line with a typical national economic growth rate of 3 per cent. You input 3 per cent for the percentage growth rate and you set up the formula to grow sales annually: ((1 + the percentage growth rate) × sales). You look at your answer and you see that sales in five years are £1,024 billion. You think to yourself that this looks wrong, so you look at your spreadsheet again. You see the percentage input clearly typed: '3', and you check the formula: ((1 + the percentage input) × sales), and that is correct too. Finally, you check that this year's sales are correct and, yes, it is £1 billion. The formula is correct and so are the inputs, so despite your initial instincts £1,024 billion must be the right answer.

Wrong. You have trusted your calculations and a program more than common sense. It turns out that, where your input was 3 per cent, the program recognized it as 300 per cent because 3 per cent is actually 0.03. When you tried to grow each year by multiplying by 1.03, you in fact multiplied by 4. Hopefully, you are thinking that there is no way you would have made this mistake. You are thinking that it is obvious that sales could not be 1,024 times larger in five years under any circumstances. This is the point. It *is* obvious, and will be even more obvious to any colleague or boss.

This is clearly an extreme example used for purposes of illustration, but a colleague of mine recently informed me of the results of a financial forecast model's annual sales figure that he had grown at 2 per cent annually (based on inflation) for five years. The result, according to his spreadsheet, was that sales had grown by 25 per cent in total. Not so obvious a mistake, but still clearly wrong, and easily avoidable with a sanity check. You must always sanity-check your spreadsheets to ensure that your analysis is robust.

In some cases, you might see that an answer looks strange but not so implausible. You need to sanity-check these numbers too. Usually, you will discover that they are also wrong, but occasionally they will be correct. If strange answers are indeed correct, you need to understand what is causing the numbers to look odd. You can bet your bottom dollar that your boss will notice any atypical answers and want to know the explanation. If you cannot provide the explanation, you will completely undermine your analysis, no matter how brilliant it is; if you have a ready explanation for such anomalies, you will look intelligent and in charge of your work.

'Buddy up' to check and debug analysis

Analysis can get very complicated. I have seen some analytical models that comprise several hundred spreadsheets. A number of investment banking first-rungers highlighted the practice of 'buddying up' with fellow analysts to check and debug each other's analysis. If you have been working on the same spreadsheet for some time, you cannot see errors clearly. A fresh pair of eyes can check and debug errors much more efficiently than you can after staring into your computer screen for hours on end. Find a colleague who is willing to 'buddy' with you, and together ensure that your, and your colleague's, analysis is rock-solid.

> A fresh pair of eyes can check and debug errors much more efficiently than you can after staring into your computer screen for hours on end.

Round numbers to one or two decimal places at the most (and be consistent)

Many numbers calculated in spreadsheets have numerous decimal places. You do not want to show all the decimal places because it looks untidy and because multiple levels of decimal places indicate a level of accuracy that is rarely appropriate for the kind of analysis performed in a business context. Round the numbers to no more than one or two decimal places at the most and make sure that you are consistent within that data set.

Adjust the largest rounded number to make sure numbers sum precisely to totals

One issue that you will encounter when you round is that the sum of the rounded numbers does not equal the exact total. If you are showing a direct spreadsheet output, eg a printed worksheet or an on-screen display, you do not need to worry about this, because it is understood that the spreadsheet is rounding the display but summing the unrounded numbers. However, if you are copying the numbers into a memo or a presentation then you do need to worry about numbers summing to the exact total, because it is not obvious whether there is a rounding error or whether you have been sloppy. The times when this is most obvious is when you sum a set of figures to 100 per cent and the rounded figures do not actually sum to 100 per cent.

Consider the three percentages 50.3 per cent, 35.3 per cent and 14.4 per cent. The sum of these is precisely 100.0 per cent. Now suppose you round them to the nearest whole number. The series becomes 50 per cent, 35 per cent and 14 per cent, which sums to 99 per cent. You have rounded down appropriately for each number but lost a whole percentage point in the process. The correct approach to solve this problem is to increase the largest number in the series, because this requires making the smallest relative adjustment. So in the above example you would write the series as 51 per cent, 35 per cent and 14 per cent, which sums correctly to 100 per cent.

Always round error bars or uncertainties to one significant figure

Recall that in scenario analysis there are often three cases, the conservative case, the base case and the aggressive case. The way these data are sometimes displayed is with error bars. For example, suppose you calculate valuations to two decimal places, with values £8.48 million, £10.18 million and £11.88 million in the conservative, base and aggressive cases respectively. You might show the data as follows: £10.18 million +/–£1.70 million. The first point to observe is that the error bars are a way of showing uncertainty in the outcome, and so it makes no sense to be too accurate. A simple rule to follow is always to round to one significant figure. In this example, the correct way to show the data is: £10 million +/– £2million.

Polish to professional presentation standards

In Chapter 4, we discuss professional finish for documents, including formatting and proofing. First-rungers are notoriously slack in polishing their work when it comes to analysis. They get carried away by the detail of the analysis and forget to add the finishing touches. You need to spend as much time editing, formatting and proofing your analytical work for presentation purposes as you do any other written work.

Kirk Williams of Chrysler remarks that he has seen colleagues presenting analysis that was superb – accurate and well organized – but
their managers pulled them up on missing footnotes, typos, and untidy
page layout. The analysis is the hard part; the editing and presentation
side is easy, although it does take time, and you should not overlook it.

In a nutshell – How to be a great research analyst

- Clarify information requests.
- Work out for yourself what question the information request is trying to answer.
- Build and leverage an 'information network'.
- Become an information node and the go-to person.
- Do not forget the internet as an additional information resource.
- Source and date your information for rigour.
- Summarize, synthesize and use the one-pager to highlight insights.
- Learn the essential quantitative methods.
- Learn the basics of spreadsheets.
- Learn the three important functions to help build spreadsheet models (IF, SUMIF and VLOOKUP).
- Use the first-runger core toolkit for advanced analytics.
- Use primary sources for greatest accuracy.
- Validate assumptions.
- Organize your analysis.
- Use multiple short formulae instead of long single formulae.
- Triangulate by applying other analytical techniques to achieve the same output.
- Sanity-check your answers to avoid stupid mistakes.
- 'Buddy up' to check and debug analysis.
- Round numbers to one or two decimal places at the most (and be consistent).

- Adjust the largest rounded number to make sure numbers sum precisely to totals.

- Always round error bars or uncertainties to one significant figure.

- Polish to professional presentation standards.

4

Learn business communication skills 1: Speaking and writing effectively

After attitude, surveyed executives highlight communication skills as the next most important set of attributes for success on the first rung. Around 60 per cent ranked them in the top category

After attitude, executives highlight communication skills as the next most important set of attributes for success on the first rung.

of importance and around 90 per cent ranked them in the top two categories of importance. What is most surprising given this result, not to mention the raft of other literature that highlights the importance of communication, is how little new executives have actually explicitly developed their communication skills. In most of your academic career, in school and university or college, you will have developed your communication skills implicitly through presentation of your homework or through class participation. Even in a professional context, while everyone recognizes the importance of communication skills, most people do little to develop their skills actively. This should not be the case. From this day on, focus on developing your communication skills at every opportunity – whenever you speak to your boss or write a memo or interact in meetings, you should be thinking about your effectiveness and how to improve it.

Communicating in a business environment is different from communicating socially, recreationally or academically. Of course, you still need to read and write; you still have conversations, including social or recreational conversations; and you still need to use elements of social communication skills. However, to be an effective business communicator, you need to learn new skills and think intelligently about your day-to-day business communication strategy.

This chapter discusses the basics of how to become an effective business communicator on the first rung and how to build the skills for future success. It focuses on the critical dos and don'ts of business communication and on speaking and writing effectively.

Critical dos and don'ts of business communication

Richard Mosely was a first-year investment banker in New York with a major Wall Street investment bank. Bankers officially call their first-rungers 'analysts', but in jest often call them 'bag-carriers', because their primary role when attending client meetings is to carry the bags containing the presentations. In other words, senior bankers expect first-rungers' contributions, particularly in client meetings, to be minimal. At one meeting, Richard and his director were advising a corporate client considering a purchase of another company. The client explained that early conversations with the target company suggested that a friendly purchase of the business might not be easy to achieve. The director paused to consider the strategic implications of this information. Richard, somewhat excited because he had only had to carry his own bag to the meeting that day, thought he had a solution to the issue. He leaned forward to the client and asked: 'Do you want to go hostile on them?' By this, he meant that the client should launch a very high-profile, potentially high-cost and certainly stressful hostile takeover. The director with whom Richard was travelling smoothly adapted to Richard's outburst and suggested that perhaps, at this time, a hostile takeover was not the wisest course of action. Then he whispered to Richard that it might also help if he did up his fly!

On the first rung, you have to learn to navigate the tricky path of making a contribution, but not overstepping your bounds. It is a matter of balance. Particularly

> You have to learn to navigate the tricky path of making a contribution, but not overstepping your bounds. It is a matter of balance.

when it comes to communicating, achieving this balance can be quite difficult. The main reason for this is that people often place the most value on someone's experience, at least in the first instance. Because you have limited experience, your viewpoint is more likely to be questioned and even your right to express it may be challenged, regardless of how valuable your contribution may be.

The following is a list of dos and don'ts that you would be wise to observe in your first-rung career.

Do listen actively – but don't remain silent

Former Harvard president Charles B Eliot once said, 'There is no mystery about successful business intercourse… Exclusive attention to the person who is speaking to you is very important. Nothing else is so flattering as that' (quoted from Dale Carnegie's *How to Win Friends and Influence People*). Eliot is right: colleagues want a rapt audience, but it is about more than making the other person feel flattered. It is important to hear what is said.

Listening is more than sitting in silence and trying to pay attention. One of the ways that many executives ensure active listening

> One of the ways that many executives ensure active listening is by asking questions.

is by asking questions. Even if the purpose of the conversation is to request an individual to do a specific job, they will begin by asking that individual what he or she thinks about the issue at hand and continue to ask clarifying questions to ensure that they understand the individual's perspective. They are able to make sure that any request is reasonable and aligned with the individual's own expectations. Ultimately, this active listening reflects well on these executives because they are able to achieve superior results.

Dan Barker of Ameritech found that he was able to differentiate himself from his peers by asking questions. Dan noticed that most first-rungers, particularly those from prestigious academic backgrounds, are afraid to ask questions because they believe they are admitting their ignorance. Dan recognized the obvious truth that first-rungers are ill informed compared with their more senior colleagues and learned that seeking out the right people and asking them questions, while remaining respectful of their time, was the key to becoming less ignorant. He was also able to build relationships because he showed humility and respect.

It is important that you listen and ask questions, but do not be too deferential – do not sit in a meeting room and nod your head in agreeable affirmation. Although Abraham Lincoln advises us that it is 'better to remain silent and be thought a fool than to open your mouth and remove all doubt', if you want to create a positive impression, rather than avoid a negative one, you must express yourself. This does not mean that you have to speak in every situation, but it does mean that you have to seek appropriate opportunities to contribute. The first challenge for a first-runger is to know when these appropriate opportunities occur. The story of Richard Mosely is a cautionary tale about speaking up inappropriately. You need to use common sense. Richard learned his lesson and became very savvy about when to speak up. If he was in a meeting where there were clients present and there was a strong flow of dialogue, he did not interject. Instead, he waited until after the meeting and made his point to his boss 'offline'. This way, Richard received credit for his thinking and timing. In internal meetings and in pre- and post-client meeting situations, Richard found lots of opportunities to make valued contributions. Eventually, he grew more confident and was able to contribute positively in client meetings.

Do express a point of view – but don't argue

While you may not have the experience of more senior colleagues, you should always try to have your own point of view. Too often, first-rungers either do not form their own views or they do not communicate them if they have them. Make sure you try to evaluate everything yourself and be sure to speak up and present your viewpoint, but choose the appropriate timing for your contribution, as we discussed earlier. While you need to establish that you are a good contributor in meetings, you must recognize, as Harriet Giggs of PricewaterhouseCoopers puts it, 'when not to press your point and when to shut up'. In particular, you must observe a very simple universal business rule: when based on the same information two or more people disagree, the prevailing opinion belongs to the most senior person. Often, that opinion will be wrong. The point is that you need to know when to back off from pressing your opinion.

A great rule of thumb is to state your point of view no more than twice. If there is still disagreement after your second attempt, back down gracefully. Further attempts will prove no more persuasive, but

> A great rule of thumb is to state your point of view no more than twice... Further attempts will prove no more persuasive, but they will brand you as argumentative.

they will brand you as argumentative. Do not believe those organizations that claim to have a non-hierarchical culture. Some cultures are less hierarchical than others, but all are hierarchical to some degree and, when it comes to disagreeing, you would be foolish to go head to head with a senior manager, even if you are right.

Do be fact-based – but don't be too detailed

As we discussed earlier, a major problem with being a first-runger is that you lack credibility because of limited experience. This is particularly true for first-rungers in consulting roles because their job specifically requires that they work in situations where they do not have as much experience as the people they are advising. The executives interviewed for this book who had been consultants felt an effective solution to overcoming a lack of credibility was to base communications on fact and limit judgement-based comments unless explicitly called for. Facts can only be disputed for their accuracy and reliability. So long as your fact base is reliably sourced, you will be able to communicate compelling arguments and robust viewpoints even if you are the most junior person in the room. One way of ensuring a commanding fact base is to control any numbers or quantitative analysis. Most bosses hate the numbers, and if you base your viewpoint on an understanding of the numbers you will be well placed to make useful contributions.

One executive who joined an investment bank employed this strategy to great effect. Having worked at another bank previously, this executive already had expertise and experience. Nevertheless, he knew that, in a new environment, he had to start from scratch and

> Most bosses hate the numbers, and if you base your viewpoint on an understanding of the numbers you will be well placed to make useful contributions.

build a reputation before he could leverage his experience. In his first months, he made sure he was on top of any financial analysis and was able to earn the confidence of his bosses. Before too long he was able to delegate the numbers to other junior staff and rely more on his experience when making contributions.

The critical thing to get right when basing your communications on a fact base is pitching your communications at the right level of detail. This is a potential stumbling block for many first-rungers, as the temptation is to be too focused on minutiae. The trick is to use the bare minimum of detail but to have at your fingertips supporting data. For example, suppose you work for a consumer product company such as Unilever and, because you control the numbers, your boss asks you how much a marketing programme is going to cost. Such a programme might include a TV and radio advertising campaign and a brand promotion strategy in stores. You could answer your boss by providing a detailed cost breakdown of the TV and radio advertising, including how many hours of airtime you are using, the cost per hour of airtime, production costs, legal costs etc, but this would be too much. All that your boss asked for was the cost of the marketing programme, so you should give him or her that number and be prepared with follow-up analysis if asked.

Sometimes, however, bosses will ask open-ended questions, where it is not possible to provide a simple headline answer. For example, they might ask you to update them on the status of a multifaceted project or on the preliminary findings of some qualitative piece of research. What is the right level of detail you should use to answer these questions? One answer is to make sure you pass the 'Elevator Test'. In the 'Elevator Test', you have to imagine that you have the same time to present your answer as it takes for a typical lift journey – about 30 seconds. This is the oral equivalent of the one-pager we discussed in Chapter 3, and similarly it is a test of your ability to hit the main themes and synthesize them crisply. Should your boss want more detail and engage you on this topic, it is important to have further detail at your fingertips.

> In the 'Elevator Test', you have to pretend that you have the same time to present your answer as it takes for a typical lift journey – about 30 seconds.

Do be to the point – but don't be blunt

An important aspect of communicating effectively, whether it is expressing a point of view, asking a question or simply sharing information, is being to the point. In one scene from the 1987 film *Planes, Trains and Automobiles*, Steve Martin launches into a tirade at John Candy for his boring stories: 'Didn't you notice on the plane when you started talking, eventually I started reading the vomit bag? Didn't that give you some sort of clue, like maybe this guy is not enjoying it?... You know, when you're telling these little stories, here's an idea... have a point! It makes it so much more interesting for the listener!'

While I doubt that colleagues will be quite so acerbic in their feedback, people who belabour their points or ramble are ineffective. Their audience tires quickly and their ability to persuade is jeopardized. Ernest Hemingway was renowned for his terse prose. He was clear and to the point, used simple language and was economical with his words. His example is one to follow in your spoken and written business communications.

A concise communication approach sometimes runs the risk of people viewing you as blunt or rude. At Harvard Business School, classes are taught in the Socratic method – the professor facilitates dialogue between the students by asking questions instead of lecturing. Harvard Business School students often remember individuals not for the quality of their comments but for the blunt manner of their delivery. The students call these individuals 'sharks' because they make their points aggressively, by attacking and contradicting classmates and, in the worst cases, belittling other students. Even in a competitive environment like Harvard Business School, this term is not a compliment. Before you speak, ask yourself: who has different views? And why? Who might be defensive? Who is affected by any implications of your viewpoint? With these insights, you can position your viewpoint appropriately.

Once you have understood the broader context, you need to modify your language to prevent bluntness. You can achieve this in many ways but, as one executive suggests, the technique employed by Benjamin Franklin is as good as any. Franklin replaced the absolutism in his views by beginning his comments with 'softeners' such as 'It appears

> Before you speak, ask yourself: who has different views? And why? Who might be defensive? Who is affected by any implications of your viewpoint?

to me' or 'If I am not mistaken', and he found that people were far more amenable to his perspective.

Do use corporate language – but don't overuse management jargon

One of the hardest things to get a grip on before you start on the first rung is the corporate language. Every firm has its specific lexicon, and most firms also use many of the same expressions and acronyms. A few examples are 'touch base', 'value added', 'drill down' and 'FYI'. Comic strips such as *Dilbert* have made an art form out of satirizing management jargon, and the reality is that most companies do use a corporate language that includes some management jargon. In defence of jargon and particularly some of the acronyms, they do have their advantages. It is a lot quicker, for example, to start an e-mail 'FYI' than to have to write out 'For your information'.

The trick to getting your business communication language right is to incorporate the company-specific corporate language and to go no further. If you start talking about 'synergies' and 'value added' when no one else in the company uses these expressions, you will not come across well. Furthermore, you should be wary of clustering jargon, because this also sounds very artificial. Consider the following sentence: 'Net, net at the end of the day, a silo approach to the business units will not optimize realizable synergies.' What this actually means is: 'If departments do not cooperate with each other, the business will not be efficient.' Even if your colleagues understand the language, they will probably be too distracted by the jargon to appreciate the message.

Do be inclusive – but don't be indiscreet

One of the many mistakes that first-rungers make is to forget to include everybody on group communications. Egos are very sensitive and nothing irritates people more than being excluded

> One of the many mistakes that first-rungers make is to forget to include everybody on group communications.

from a communication even if it is only remotely relevant to them. In my own career, I was reprimanded on a number of occasions for not copying someone on an e-mail or forgetting to invite someone to a meeting. On one occasion, I had worked for over two months on a project and had forwarded, by e-mail, a large presentation to my client and copied it to the presentation team. One individual, whose sum contribution to the work had been to attend the initial meeting for one hour, strongly requested that, in the future, I always include him on all major correspondence with the client. Obviously, this kind of politicking is unpleasant, but, when it comes down to it, you will lose nothing by being inclusive when you are on the first rung. Where possible, always try to keep people happy with you. We will spend more time on office politics later in the book but, for now, remember that, for any major communication, you best serve your career by keeping everyone in the loop, whether they are central or tangential.

There is a big difference between keeping people in the loop who are legitimately affiliated with a piece of work or issue, however loosely, and sharing information with the wrong people. It is a criminal offence in securities law to share 'inside information' with anyone who is not an insider without adhering to very strict protocols. Even within a company, often an explicit process exists around internal company communications to ensure that the right people hear the right information at the right time and in the right way. For example, reorganizations are often fraught with tension, not least because they usually come with lay-offs, reshuffles and demotions, and senior management are keen to ensure that employees hear a consistent and reliable message on potential changes. Jack Reardon of American Medical Security always double-checks the distribution list after rereading his communications to make sure that he has included everyone who should be included and no one who should not be. Jim Taylor of Merrill Lynch even checks with someone senior if he is in doubt on who should and who should not be included on a distribution list. As Jim puts it, 'You don't want to be known for being someone who cannot handle sensitive information.'

You don't want to be known for being someone who cannot handle sensitive information.

Speaking effectively in business

One of the very first things your bosses and colleagues will notice is how well you speak. People are conscious of listening to a good speaker but they are even more aware of listening to a bad speaker. We discuss the key elements of speaking well in different forums

> One of the very first things your bosses and colleagues will notice is how well you speak.

in Chapter 5, but here are four important principles that you need to observe to be an effective first-rung speaker in all business situations.

Be natural

Many people find it hard to be natural when they are speaking in certain business settings, such as to a superior or a group of colleagues, and, while a business conversation needs to differ from a social conversation in many ways, they both work best if you are natural. Carl Moran of General Electric believes that his ability to speak effectively comes from being comfortable with himself and not trying to force a preconceived speaking style. Unfortunately, although you can actively try to adopt many of the strategies and tactics discussed in this book, actively trying to be natural is a bit like trying not to think of the colour green: the result is the very opposite of the desired outcome!

The trick to speaking naturally is to start out as if you were speaking in a normal social situation. If you are speaking to an audience, then you introduce yourself as if you were meeting someone for the first time. If you are speaking one to one and are familiar with the person, begin by asking how he or she is and using the person's name just as you would with a friend.

Show confidence

What is the difference between an introverted librarian and an extroverted librarian? When speaking to you, an introverted librarian stares at his or her feet while an extroverted librarian stares at your feet. Nothing is more uncomfortable than listening to people mumble incoherently into their or even your shoes. If you are unable to show confidence when you speak, your own credibility is undermined. If you are sharing information, your audience may doubt the accuracy and reliability of the information; if you are presenting a point of view, it may question your conviction; and if you are asking a question, it may worry about your competence.

How do you show confidence if you do not feel confident? First, we need to be very clear on what we mean by showing confidence in the context of speaking in a

> Showing confidence when speaking is about believing in what you are saying and believing in your authority to say it.

business environment. Showing confidence when speaking is about believing in what you are saying and believing in your authority to say it. Confidence, therefore, comes from preparation and hard work. So long as you know your stuff, you should be fine. No one can legitimately doubt you if you are fact-based and have your facts researched and validated.

Beyond ensuring that you are fully prepared, you can employ a couple of simple techniques to embolden yourself and make yourself appear confident. Look your audience directly in the eye frequently (not continuously), and speak deliberately with a clear, audible voice. Even if you are a jangling bag of nerves inside, with these two techniques you will at least appear confident.

Begin with the nugget

As a first-runger, your opportunity to speak at length is limited. When you speak, make sure that you get the nugget, the key message, out straight away. Imagine the following: you are involved in helping your boss with a divisional reorganization. You have heard gossip in the division and know people are talking about how the division is going to change and discussing which employees are going to be fired and which are going to be promoted. Because such speculation and uncertainty are bad for morale, you believe it is important that your boss should begin a comprehensive communication programme to everyone in the division. How would you convey this message to your boss? If I were in this situation, I would say something like: 'We should communicate the divisional reorganization to the staff as soon as possible.' I would start with the nugget – the most important piece of information to convey. I would not start by building up my argument as I did in this paragraph, because I know that if I do not get to the nugget straight away I may be interrupted and never get there. In other words, I would do the opposite of what you are

> Start with the nugget or conclusion and provide the fact-based rationale afterwards as time permits.

taught in school. Start with the nugget or conclusion and provide the fact-based rationale afterwards as time permits.

Use people's first names

Mike Sandler learned all the names of the people in the administrative department because he recognized, as Dale Carnegie puts it in *How to Win Friends and Influence People*, that 'the average person is more interested in his or her own name than in all the other names on earth put together'. Next time you are talking to someone who is a professional salesperson, listen to how many times he or she uses your name and contrast this usage with everyone else's. You will notice a striking difference. Salespeople begin almost every sentence with your name. They can overdo it and engender mistrust because it appears too contrived, but you should have no doubt that using people's first names is the best way to hold their attention.

Not everyone has Mike's memory for names. Some executives use tools such as flash cards and similar devices to help them memorize names. While you never want to be discovered using this trick, it is a great one to employ. It does not matter what method you use, but it is important that you are able to remember people's names.

Professional business writing

Most first-rungers come into their first job thinking that they write well. After all, they have had a whole education where writing was the main medium for expressing their learning and knowledge through papers and written exams. However, just as speaking well socially does not necessarily translate into speaking well in a business environment, so writing well academically does not necessarily translate into writing well in a business setting. Luis Costa of Procter & Gamble recalls that, despite his having been an excellent writer at college, his boss edited his first memo many, many times before she was finally happy with it.

In this section, we discuss the essentials of writing well in the workplace, and in the next chapter we cover some of the subtleties of writing across different written communication media such as e-mails and memos.

Use a clear structure

Pick up an old paper that you wrote in school or college and look at the structure. Probably you will find a title and a series of paragraphs, starting with an introduction, then running through the main points and arguments and finally culminating in a conclusion. If someone wants to understand your paper and its main points, they have to read the whole paper from start to finish. Few business people have time to read everything they receive thoroughly, which is why a well-written business communication should allow someone to scan it and get the key messages without having to wade through the detail.

You need to think about two aspects of document structure: 1) the logical structure – how you organize your points; and 2) the visual structure – how you format and display the document.

Of the two, logical structure is the harder to master. It is beyond the bounds of this book to discuss how to write with logical structure. However, several executives recommended the following two books: *The Pyramid Principle* by Barbara Minto and *Elements of Style* by William Strunk Jr and EB White.

While much easier to master, visual structure is no less important. Do not be one of those purists who think that the substance of what they say or write is all that matters. Even if your documents' logical organization is perfect, if their visual structure is poor they will still lack clarity. One of my old bosses used to tell me that visual presentation was more important than substance. He argued that, if you did not present a piece of work well, no one would bother reading it.

Figure 4.1 shows an example of unformatted business writing and Figure 4.2 one of formatted business writing.

Figure 4.1 contains the same points as Figure 4.2, but is much harder to read and comprehend because there is no visual structure. Figure 4.2 is much clearer because it has paragraphs, spaced sentences, delineated points and bolded text.

You need to think about visual structure and format in more than just written documents. Look at the two sets of financial analysis in Figure 4.3. Just as with Figures 4.1 and 4.2, the formatted version in Figure 4.3 is much clearer than the unformatted version. You can

> A well-written business communication should allow someone to scan it and get the key messages without having to wade through the detail.

Hi Mary
Hope all is well. Just wanted to update you on the meeting we had earlier with the fabric supplier. Overall, the meeting went well. The supplier seems willing to negotiate on price, but it depends on how big our order is. They offer big discounts on orders over 1,000 square feet. The supplier is experiencing delays in obtaining indigo and yellow dyes. They will arrive two weeks later than the other dyes due for delivery next Wednesday the 14th. The supplier also expressed interest in providing us with buttons. I did not make any commitments but said I would go back to you. I suggest you and I meet to discuss these points. Could you give the supplier a call to see if we can get some discount for the late delivery of the dyes? I will schedule a follow-up meeting with you and the supplier for Monday to finalize price and to discuss buttons.
What are your thoughts?
Regards
Stuart

Figure 4.1 *Unformatted writing sample*

Hi Mary

Hope all is well.

Just wanted to update you on the meeting we had earlier with the fabric supplier.

Overall, the meeting went well. The following were the **key points to emerge**:

1. The supplier seems willing to negotiate on price, but it depends on how big our order is. They offer big discounts on orders over 1,000 square feet.

2. The supplier is experiencing delays in obtaining indigo and yellow dyes. They will arrive two weeks later than the other dyes due for delivery next Wednesday the 14th.

3. The supplier expressed interest in providing us with buttons.

I did not make any commitments but said I would go back to you.

I suggest the following **next steps**:

1. You and I meet to discuss these points.

2. You give the supplier a call to see if we can get some discount for the late delivery of the dyes.

3. I schedule a follow-up meeting with you and the supplier for Monday to finalize price and to discuss buttons.

What are your thoughts?

Regards

Stuart

Figure 4.2 *Formatted writing sample*

Unformatted income statement (£m)	
Revenues	100
Cost of goods sold	50
Gross earnings	50
Sales and general admin costs	20
Depreciation	10
Earnings before interest and tax	20
Interest payments	10
Earnings before tax	10
Tax	3
Net earnings	7

Formatted income statement (£m)	
Revenues	*100*
Cost of goods sold	50
Gross earnings	*50*
Sales and general admin costs	20
Depreciation	10
Earnings before interest and tax	*20*
Interest payments	10
Earnings before tax	*10*
Tax	3
Net earnings	7

Figure 4.3   *Unformatted and formatted income statements*

scan the formatted income statement and find any line items quickly, because the visual structure provides easy points of reference. Techniques such as highlighting with bold or italicized text and spacing are as valid for formatting numbers as they are for formatting text.

Ensure consistency

In creative writing, expressing the same thing in different terms is an art. Look at the following extract from Shakespeare's *Richard II* (Act 2, Scene 1):

> *This royal throne of kings, this sceptred isle,*
> *This earth of majesty, this seat of Mars,*
> *This other Eden, demi-paradise,*
> *This fortress built by Nature for herself*
> *Against infection and the hand of war,*
> *This happy breed of men, this little world,*
> *This precious stone set in the silver sea,*
> *Which serves it in the office of a wall*
> *Or as a moat defensive to a house,*
> *Against the envy of less happier lands.*
> *This blessed plot, this earth, this realm, this England.*

Shakespeare writes poetically, beautifully and evocatively, but if he wrote like this in business memos he would not go far. Written business communication is not meant to be artistic. It is meant to be factual and clear and, therefore, requires internal consistency. If this extract were rewritten for a business memo, here is how it would look: 'England'. And every other time the memo referred to England, it would use the word 'England'. Obviously, this is a bit of an extreme illustration, but many words frequently connote the same thing or meaning in business, for example companies use a number of other words to refer to sales, eg 'revenues', 'contribution' and 'top line'. Don't be tempted to switch and change your terminology; use the same terminology throughout and avoid confusing your audience.

In my first job, a managing director told me, 'I don't care if you make mistakes, so long as you are internally consistent.' The point he was making was not that mistakes do not matter, but that if, in a single document, you have multiple versions of a single number, for example, it is much worse than having the same wrong number everywhere; it shows sloppiness and lack of professionalism. A consistent mistake, on the other hand, you can often justifiably explain, eg in terms of a poor source.

In addition to terminology, the other most important dimensions of internal consistency are formatting, tense and voice. As we discussed above, formatting is important for providing visual structure. Consistent formatting is important to make it easy for the reader to navigate the document. It is also a mark of professionalism. Consistency is also the most important thing to get right with tense. Finally, you can use either the active or passive voice. In the active voice, a clear subject precedes every verb, for example: 'Consumers spend more money in an environment of low interest rates.' In the passive voice, the subject follows the verb or is even implicit: 'More money is spent (by consumers) in an environment of low interest rates.' In general, most people prefer the active voice because of its simplicity and clarity. The passive voice is more dispassionate and academic. Both have their uses, but – make sure that you are consistent!

Proof everything!

If one mark of unprofessional writing stands above all others, it

If one mark of unprofessional writing stands above all others, it is typos – spelling mistakes, repeated words, missing words etc.

is typos – spelling mistakes, repeated words, missing words etc. You may have written the masterpiece of all memos – insightful, logically structured, compelling in its conclusions and internally consistent – but if it is full of typos you will be regarded as sloppy, and the work, brilliant as it may be, will be discounted. Bankers tend to be the best at proofing documents because they are, simply put, the most anal; even senior bankers take great pains to spot typos. When I was a banker, one director bet me a bottle of champagne that he would find at least 10 typos in a 100-page document that I had prepared for submission to a European government privatization department. Those bankers who contributed to this book agree that you need to follow a disciplined procedure to ensure your documents are professionally finished:

1. Set aside some real time to proof properly; definitely do not consider proofing a quick skim-reading exercise.
2. Make sure you print out hard copies of your work to proof, and never proof on a computer screen because you will miss a lot of typos.
3. Clearly mark up the corrections to the hard copy and wait to make any changes on-screen until you have marked up the entire copy.
4. Make the changes to the electronic copy.
5. Print off the corrected electronic version, and go through the paper mark-up and the corrected version side by side with a different colour of pen or pencil (for clarity) and tick off every single mark-up that has been appropriately corrected. Any that you have missed, mark up on the new master for correction.
6. Repeat the process until your master has no mark-ups.
7. Finally, particularly if you are proofing an important document, find a quiet room and reread the master out loud word for word to ensure no other typos have crept in during proofing and as a final sense check.

Obviously, proofing is deadly dull and it requires discipline to do it properly, but, I promise, you will be well served to build a reputation for having excellent attention to detail.

In a nutshell – How to learn business communication skills 1

- Do listen actively – but don't remain silent.

- Do express a point of view – but don't argue.

- Do be fact-based – but don't be too detailed.

- Do be to the point – but don't be blunt.

- Do use corporate language – but don't overuse management jargon.

- Do be inclusive – but don't be indiscreet.

- Learn to speak effectively:

  - Be natural.

  - Show confidence.

  - Begin with the nugget.

  - Use people's first names.

- Learn to write effectively:

  - Use a clear structure.

  - Ensure consistency.

  - Proof everything!

5

Learn business communication skills 2: The 10 key areas

'Learn business communication skills 2' picks up where 'Learn business communication skills 1' left off. In particular it covers tips for the 10 areas of communication, and tailoring your personal communication strategy.

Tips for the 10 different areas of communication

While most communication is either spoken (including associated body language) or written, there are a number of areas that require subtle differences in the ways that you handle them. In this section, we discuss 10 forums of business communication, as shown in Figure 5.1, and the main things you need to do to be effective in each of them. Other areas of communications are not discussed here, but if you can handle these 10 you will have all the skills required to cope with any other form of business communication that is not highly specialized.

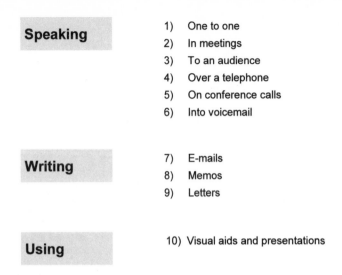

Speaking	1) One to one
	2) In meetings
	3) To an audience
	4) Over a telephone
	5) On conference calls
	6) Into voicemail
Writing	7) E-mails
	8) Memos
	9) Letters
Using	10) Visual aids and presentations

Figure 5.1 *The 10 main forums of business communication*

1 Speaking one to one

You need to handle two main types of one-to-one interactions. The first is the formal one-to-one interaction, such as a meeting in the boss's office to discuss a new project, and the second is the informal one-to-one interaction, the kind that might take place in the corridor or with someone stopping by your desk. We first focus on the formal meeting, where the following are among the most important things to get right.

Always have an agenda prepared

An agenda is a list of discussion topics that provide structure to meetings. Agendas are important because they set the scope and objectives of a meeting and focus the discussion towards them.

> Agendas are important because they set the scope and objectives of a meeting and focus the discussion towards them.

Mark Jackson of Dell argues that, without an agenda, the meeting is just a chat where little is achieved. Figure 5.2 shows an example of a typical agenda for a kick-off meeting (initial meeting to get the project up and running) for a new project.

> ➤ Meeting objectives

> ➤ Project overview

> ➤ Project objectives

> ➤ Deliverables and deadlines

> ➤ Next steps

Figure 5.2 *Example of an agenda for a project team kick-off meeting*

As you can see, agendas need not be complicated, just a short concise list covering the key elements of the meeting. The first item, 'Meeting objectives', is a very useful way to begin the meeting, as it details exactly the purpose and goals of the meeting and lets everybody know why they are there.

Regardless of who set the meeting, always have an agenda ready. You may not need to use it if your counterpart scheduled the meeting and has been diligent in preparing the agenda, but you will look very sharp if you do need to take control. If you have scheduled the meeting, you will be expected to control the agenda. If you want to look very professional, you should type up an agenda and make copies. Sometimes, a typed agenda is too formal. Referring to an agenda written in your notebook is more relaxed and more appropriate for some situations, but still shows good organization and professionalism. For short meetings with simple agendas, Tom Brent of Disney suggests having the agenda items ready in your head and mentioning them at the beginning of the meeting or writing them down on a flip chart or whiteboard.

Warm up with pleasantries

One of the more unfortunate aspects of the business world is that people get so focused on their job that they forget to be human. Do not make the mistake of walking into a meeting room, sitting down, proudly pulling out your agenda and diving right into it without at least saying hello and asking how

> Do not make the mistake of walking into a meeting room, sitting down, proudly pulling out your agenda and diving right into it without at least saying hello and asking how the other person is doing.

the other person is doing. It does not take much time – a simple 'How are you?' can be sufficient social lubrication – but the reward comes in the form of more receptive, cooperative meetings and better long-term relationships. If you work frequently with people, you should try to get to know more about them beyond their working lives. If you do not know the other person, then discuss safe subjects such as weather, travel or sports, all of which serve as useful standbys for conversation in such situations. As we discuss later in the book, showing a genuine interest in other people is very important in building an effective network.

Establish the time-frame and stick to it

Before you get into the agenda, Harriet Giggs of Pricewaterhouse-Coopers suggests asking how long the other person has available. Even if you scheduled a specific period of time, people's diaries often shift or things come up, so

> Even if you scheduled a specific period of time, people's diaries often shift or things come up, so it is always worth checking how much time they have.

it is always worth checking how much time they have. Moreover, it is a matter of professional courtesy too often overlooked. Whatever the answer, you should try to stick to it – remember you are the junior. If you do need more time than is offered, schedule a follow-up meeting or negotiate a longer time-frame at the start of the meeting.

Use time checks

For Kirk Williams of Chrysler, a good way to ensure that the meeting stays on track and accomplishes the objectives of the agenda in the time-frame allotted is to check the time. In social environments it is rude to look at your watch when talking with someone, but if you look at the time openly and say something like 'I am conscious that we only have a few more minutes; perhaps we could focus on X or Y', you will be respected for your professional courtesy and for your constructive focus.

Conclude with a summary of agreed actions and next steps

Every meeting has a beginning and an end, and at the end of every meeting you should summarize anything that was agreed and next steps. A summary provides a natural wrap-up and ensures that both of you leave the meeting clear on actions and responsibilities. If you have taken good notes, it is easy to glance through them and reel off the important items that will require attention. If you have controlled the agenda, it is your responsibility to summarize. Even if you have not controlled the agenda, be ready to provide the summary, if your counterpart does not.

The informal one-to-one interaction is the closest to normal social conversation and so does not merit much discussion here except for one piece of advice. When speaking with someone more senior informally, the conversation is often very casual, and you should also be casual and sociable (no one likes people who take themselves too seriously), but you should always be on your guard, for the conversation can often abruptly switch tracks and become focused on a business issue. George Malone of Goldman Sachs notes that it is very easy to relax too much. He argues that you can easily lose composure if suddenly put on the spot. He suggests that you should be sociable, but always have at the back of your mind the information or answers your boss may suddenly seek.

You should also take care not to come across badly in these informal interactions. Lots of first-rungers have a habit of saying stupid things in social interactions because they let their guard down. They demean colleagues, show immaturity or appear overconfident, usually without meaning to, because they get carried away in banter.

2 Speaking in meetings

All the principles that we discussed for formal one-to-one interactions are more than sufficient to equip you with the basic capability to

> If you are responsible for running a meeting, take charge!

run meetings where more than two people are present. One piece of advice is critical: if you are responsible for running a meeting, take charge! Many first-rungers are too timid when it comes to running a meeting. They know that they are the most junior in the room and that it typically is not their place to lead discussions. It does not matter that you are junior. You are charged with managing the process for the meeting, not making the decisions. You must do all the things we discussed above and set the agenda for the meeting; you must manage the time and use time checks to make sure the meeting progresses to schedule; and you must do all these things authoritatively. Ironically, you will find that the meeting participants will appreciate you taking charge and providing the structure for the meeting. They will not think you are overstepping your bounds because you are doing your job.

Often, however, as a first-runger you will be no more than a participant. What you need to navigate, even if you are only a participant, is the interpersonal dynamics – these are vastly more complex than in a one-to-one meeting. As the first-runger in the room, you need to handle yourself particularly adroitly, because you will be the least experienced and your freedom will be less than that of more experienced attendees.

When I asked the high-flying executives interviewed for this book about performing in meetings, those who were graduates of Harvard Business School referred to their experiences of participating in case study lessons as useful preparation. If you attend a Harvard Business School class full of new students, you will notice a staccato, incoherent stream of comments as they all scramble to get noticed by the professor and get in their rehearsed comments. If you attend the same class a couple of months later, you will notice a very different pattern of student commentary. By then, the comments flow smoothly from one to the next. Successive students directly respond to and build on previous comments. This ability to contribute to the flow of discussion in a meeting is critical. Melissa Castle of Honeywell can spot Harvard Business School graduates in a meeting by the way they introduce their comments. They say things like 'Building on Jackie's point, I think...' or 'I'd like to add to what Peter said.' They refer to people who spoke by name, and their actual comments are brief, to the point and relevant. Invariably, they come across very well in meetings.

If you follow this pattern of contribution, referring to and building on previous comments, you will find your participation is more credible, not least because you are implicitly flattering those whom you refer to, making them more supportive. Obviously, if you are contradicting someone, you need to be extremely careful. As discussed earlier, use 'softeners', be respectful and remain fact-based.

3 Speaking to an audience

The most intimidating aspect of the job for many first-rungers is speaking to an audience or public speaking. Most people, in fact, are afraid of speaking in front of an audience. If you are afflicted by a fear of public speaking, you will want to work to overcome this fear or at least learn to cope with it, because you cannot avoid public speaking if you want to graduate from the first rung. If you can become a polished speaker, it is a very noticeable skill and one that can differentiate you from many of your peers. I am not going to spend much time discussing how to speak effectively to an audience, because so much other material exists on this subject that you can refer to (eg *The Art of Public Speaking* by Stephen Lucas) and because the principles we have discussed earlier actually cover much of what you need to know.

The best way to master public speaking is to practise. FE Smith once said of Winston Churchill: 'He has devoted the best years of his life to preparing his impromptu speeches.' A number of organizations provide public speaking opportunities. Probably the most ubiquitous is Toastmasters (whose website is http://www.toastmasters.org). Most major cities have at least one Toastmasters group and charge a very affordable fee. I have belonged to three different Toastmasters clubs in the last 10 years and found that their membership included a range of standards from beginners to some truly skilled speakers. The climate in Toastmasters meetings is highly supportive, and members are great at providing coaching. You can even video yourself speaking.

> If you can become a polished public speaker, it is a very noticeable skill and one that can differentiate you from many of your peers.

4 Speaking over the telephone

As with one-to-one interactions, telephone conversations can be informal or formal. All the principles that apply to formal one-to-one interactions should also apply if they are handled over the phone. However, although many telephony systems now include name and number recognition, the big difference with speaking over the telephone is that you often do not know who is calling. This is why it is standard practice to have a professional greeting for all phone calls. You will not convey a very good impression if you pick up the phone with a sleepy voice and croak a monosyllabic greeting or if your greeting is flustered and confused. One of the things to look for when you join a company is the way your colleagues answer the phone. You will probably notice a consistent greeting that you too should use (more on adopting your organization's communication culture later). In a number of US firms, for example, the greeting is often 'Hi, this is Tim' or 'Hi, you are through to Tim.' In Germany, employees at a number of firms greet simply by stating their surname. If Boris Becker were answering the phone, he would say 'Becker.' Perhaps because I am British, I always start out with 'Hello, Hugh Karseras speaking', often to the amusement of my US colleagues and friends. If you do recognize the number or the name of the person calling, then you should pick up and say something like 'Hi, Paul, how are you? What can I do for you?'

The other thing to watch out for when speaking over the telephone is using humour. It is harder to read humour if you cannot see the person, and the danger of misinterpretation is high, particularly if you do not know the other person that well. This is especially true with sarcasm! In this era of heightened sensitivity, you must watch what you say, as misconstrued jokes can have severe ramifications.

5 Speaking on conference calls

Conference calls are formal meetings that have the added twist of being conducted over the phone. All the principles that we have discussed for one-to-one and larger meetings apply here, but you should know a couple of additional points of protocol. You should ensure that you know the technical side of setting up conference calls, because everyone always looks to the first-runger in the room to get the conference call running. You need to be able to handle two types of conference calls: 1) where you conference other participants in through your phone; and 2) where you set up an external conference call with a dial-in number and pass-codes for the participants. Either way, be sure that you know what to do; it is embarrassing to be fumbling around with the technology. If you do not know who is setting up the call, assume it is you. Always bring dial-in numbers with you, even to the boss's office if you are doing the call from there. When you join the conference call, you should introduce yourself, and each time you speak, unless you are all familiar with the others' voices, you should preface your comment by saying who you are.

6 Speaking into voicemail

Voicemail is essentially an automated electronic answering machine, which allows you to do things like record a message and send it to many different people at once. If your job requires that you be proficient on voicemail, the first thing to master is the technical side of how to use voicemail. You will most likely have some kind of induction, but often this is rushed and you do not pick up all you need to know. Make sure you have access to a technical guide so that, at a minimum, you can learn how to:

■ record a greeting – what someone will hear if you are on the phone or away from your desk when they call you or when they access your voicemail directly (you can opt to leave a different message for each case if you wish);
■ record, edit and delete an outgoing message;
■ delete incoming messages that you have already heard;
■ send a message to multiple people;
■ forward a message that has been sent to you;
■ skip or quickly erase messages you do not need to hear (saving yourself time).

When sending a voicemail to one or more people, the same principles apply as for writing. It should be structured, focused and brief. The best practices that have emerged from talking to prolific users of voicemails are as follows.

Prepare a rough script
Before you record a message, particularly if it is going to convey much information, spend a few moments jotting down the key points you want to cover to ensure that your message is structured and focused.

Begin with an introduction and brief agenda
The first part of the message should tell the audience who is sending the message, who the recipients are and what the agenda is for the message. For example, the introduction might run like this: 'Hi, this is Jeremy Franks with a message for Sally Roscoe, Bill Thompson and Roger Walker on the Fisher account. Specifically, I want to update you all on the marketing plan, the budget proposal and the meeting for

next week.' Although the voicemail system automatically indicates to the recipient who sent the voicemail and at what time before it plays a message, many people skip through these introductions because they take up too much time.

Close by repeating your name and leaving contact details

I guarantee that you will receive many messages where people leave their contact number or e-mail address and you have to go back and listen to the message again to catch the full number or e-mail address. It is frustrating and a waste of time. You can avoid doing this to others by repeating your name (recipients might not have caught it properly in your introduction) and then leaving your contact details twice, speaking very clearly. An eloquent way to do this is to say something like: 'Once again, this is Jeremy Franks, and you can reach me on 212 457 1399. Let me repeat that for you; that is 212 457 1399.' Say the numbers slowly enough so that someone can understand them.

For long or important voicemails, listen to the entire message before sending

When George Malone of Goldman Sachs leaves important voicemails, or is sending a voicemail with a large distribution list, he listens to the entire message to ensure that it sounds clear and professional. This is like proofing a written document and it similarly ensures professionalism in your oral communication. Similarly, if you are leaving a long voicemail, it is wise to listen to it to make sure that it is clear and concise.

7 Writing e-mails

E-mail is now a universal forum for communication in almost all businesses. Consequently, it is also the main forum to showcase your writing skills and general intelligence. One way you can build your reputation is to CC (see below) senior colleagues on critical e-mails (eg an e-mail synthesizing the results of an important piece of analysis) sent to your direct boss, so long as the substance of the e-mail is relevant to them. Get the balance right here – you should not pepper anyone with multiple e-mails either directly or via CC. Err on the side of using this approach only for the most important e-mails.

Also remember – even if you are whipping up a quick e-mail, do not neglect to be disciplined. E-mails are frequently forwarded and you should note that everything you write is a potential reflection of the quality of your thought processes and output. Finally, be sure to understand the functionality of your e-mail program and follow all the principles we discussed in 'Professional business writing' in Chapter 4. However, you need to think about a few more things when using e-mail.

> E-mails are frequently forwarded and you should note that everything you write is a potential reflection of the quality of your thought processes and output.

Categorize and order the e-mail recipients

You will notice that most e-mail systems have two and sometimes three addressee bars – 'To', 'CC' and sometimes 'BCC'. The 'To' bar is for primary recipients of the e-mail – those whom the e-mail directly addresses. 'CC' stands for 'carbon copy' (from the old days of using carbon copy paper) and is used for people who need to be kept in the communication flow but are not directly addressed in the e-mail. The lists of recipients in the 'To' and 'CC' bars are visible to all recipients. The third bar, 'BCC' ('blind carbon copy'), is used to copy people in on an e-mail secretly – their names are not visible to the other recipients and they will not be picked up if any recipient 'Replies to All'.

When sending an e-mail to multiple colleagues, you should also think about the order in which you list them. You have two choices: order by seniority or alphabetically by surname. If you do order by seniority, be sure to get it right, and where you come across executives with equivalent ranks you should then follow alphabetical order. The safest bet is usually to adopt an alphabetical order. It is silly and a bit sad too, but you will be surprised at how many people get irritated if they come last or if their order in the list is not commensurate with their position. Having a clear and simple ordering system is the way to bypass these petty reactions.

> You will be surprised at how many people get irritated if they come last or if their order in the list is not commensurate with their position.

Be careful on the 'Reply' and 'Reply All' buttons

You will encounter numerous poor fools who have hit 'Reply All' when they meant to reply only to the sender. Usually these individuals write something innocuous, but every once in a while people write something they regret. This is particularly a risk for people who use the mouse to click on the e-mail header in their inbox, because it is easy to select the e-mail header above or below the intended one. It is far safer to use the keystroke 'Alt R' after scrolling through the inbox using the arrow keys.

I remember one e-mail from a colleague who replied to an e-mail announcing the release of Blackberries to certain staff. He hit 'Reply All' by mistake and told over 500 people, including the entire senior management, that he did not want a Blackberry because he had even less interest in e-mailing with directors at the weekend than he did talking to them on their mobile phones. The poor fellow was mortified, and to this day many of his colleagues regard him as 'the guy that sent that e-mail'. Do not be that person. Also watch out for the 'Reply' button. Some e-mail systems incorporate group addresses. Even if you hit only the 'Reply' button to a group address, your e-mail still goes to everyone in the group list. One student at Harvard Business School accidentally sent an intimate e-mail intended for his wife to his entire section, over 70 people. You can imagine his embarrassment. Take time after every e-mail before you send it, just as Jack Reardon of American Medical Security does when ensuring that he has been inclusive but not indiscreet. If you do accidentally send an e-mail that you wish you had not, some e-mail systems allow you to recall it. Be sure to learn this functionality; it could be a job-saver.

Zip large attachments and send multiple attachments separately

One of the greatest advantages of e-mail is file sharing. However, particularly for remote users who use dial-up to access the company e-mail network, large attachments take ages to download and can often crash e-mail systems. Use a zip file (a file compression utility) to minimize the size of the attachment, and if you are sending multiple attachments separate them into a series of e-mails. Several small e-mails are less likely to crash a remote user's computer than one huge e-mail. Ideally, if you are sending a large attachment you should find out if anyone will be receiving your e-mail remotely, in which case you may want to discuss sending the e-mail at a more convenient time.

Respond rapidly to impress

Sometimes it is difficult, particularly if you receive multiple e-mails every day, but you should try to respond to e-mails as fast as possible. Responding quickly is a great way to look good.

Do not forward jokes

You will receive many e-mail jokes in your career. Do not become known as 'the joke forwarder'. There is nothing wrong with having a bit of fun in the office, so long as you remain appropriate in content and timing, but let other people be the source of jokes and non-professional e-mails. You want to be seen as the professional, not the class clown. A sense of humour is an asset, but remember that you are in a place of work, not a comedy club.

Treat e-mails like any other professional written work

Because you can write e-mails quickly and even hold conversations over e-mail systems, do not be too loose with your writing. Do not forget to be structured; it is a pain for the reader to have to wade through 10 lines of small-font, single-spaced text. A little spacing and use of bullets, highlighting etc make the key messages much clearer. Avoid using things like happy faces and slang e-mail or mobile phone texting language such as 'U R Gr8' ('You are great'). Be sure to proof your e-mails, print them before you send them and follow the same proofing procedure as discussed in 'Professional business writing' in Chapter 4. Remember, everything that you write on e-mail is saved by the organization as a matter of law. In the event of any kind of litigation or regulatory enquiry, lawyers will pore over e-mail histories, and you will want to make sure that you are absolutely clean and professional.

8 Writing memos

A memo can be a note used to convey information, a record of events such as the minutes of a meeting, or an informal letter to a group of colleagues, one that does not require a signature. Writing a good memo is no different from writing a good e-mail. By nature, memos tend to be more formal and require headers and more structure than e-mails, but the principles we have discussed in the 'Writing e-mails' section above and the 'Professional business writing' section in Chapter 4 should be sufficient to apply to good memo writing. As with e-mails, be sure to pay attention to the ordering of the recipient list for the memo. Sending memos can be done via hard copy, eg through the internal (or external) mail system, or via the e-mail system. It does not matter which you choose unless your firm has a set practice. Otherwise, it depends on the time-critical nature of the memo. If not time-critical, a hard copy is more convenient for the reader, as most people print off memos to read if they receive them electronically, and you can save them the bother.

Memos, by necessity, vary in length, but the most effective memos are written on one page, just as the best synthesis of research is limited to one page, as discussed in Chapter 3. Ronald Reagan always asked for 'one-pagers' during his presidency because he wanted concise summaries that contained only the essential points of what he needed to know. If you absolutely have to write more than one page, then one effective way to keep the benefit of the one-pager is to write all the main points on the first page and then provide the details behind each of the main points on subsequent pages. This way, readers can delve deeper on specific points at their choosing.

> If you have to write more than one page... write all the main points on the first page and then provide the details behind each of the main points on subsequent pages.

9 Writing business letters

Business letters are the most formal of writing forums because they are usually sent to other companies, such as clients or business partners, and require a certain tone of professional distance. To write effective business letters, you should adhere to the following.

Focus on logical structure not visual structure
While you still need to structure your letters logically, you have less scope to play with the visual structure because business letters typically follow a more traditional paragraph structure. Try to minimize use of such visual structure devices as highlighting, bullets and changes in font.

Write in the first person plural
Whenever sending any communication outside of your company and writing about actions your company is going to take, use the first person plural. In other words, use 'we' instead of 'I'. The reason for this is

because you are writing on behalf of your colleagues not on your own behalf.

Refer to companies as though they were individuals

While 'company' in English-language terms is a collective noun, a company is also a legal entity and therefore requires third person singular grammar. Very few executives get this one right and you will frequently find executives switching back and forth between singular and plural without realizing. For example, always write: 'General Electric *is* the largest, most successful conglomerate in the world', not 'General Electric *are* the largest, most successful conglomerate in the world.' You should also refer to General Electric as an 'it' and not a 'they' or a 'them'.

Use formal company stationery

Most companies have their own letterhead paper specifically for external letters. The paper has the company address already printed on to it. Always use letterhead paper and company envelopes when sending business letters externally.

Do not forget the recipient's name, title, address and the date

Standard business letter-writing practice is to write your name and your organization's address in the top right corner of the page, aligned with the right side of the margin (the right side of the text aligns vertically). The recipient's name, title and address should appear below your name and organization's address on the left side of the page, aligned with the left margin (the left side of the text aligns vertically). The date should be written one space below the recipient's address, on the right side of the page and, as with your name and your organization's address, aligned with the right margin. An example is shown in Figure 5.3.

Get someone senior to review your letters

Whenever you deal with parties external to your organization, you need to enforce an even higher level of quality control on your work than normal. You should ask your boss or someone else senior to have a quick look through any letters you are sending out as a final 'sanity check'.

> Ask your boss or someone else senior to have a quick look through any letters you are sending out as a final 'sanity check'.

```
                                                    Lois Lane
                                                    Reporter
                                              The Daily Planet
                                                   Metropolis
  JR Ewing, President
  Ewing Oil
  South Fork
  Dallas
  Texas
                                                 4 July 1987


  Dear Mr Ewing
```

Figure 5.3   *Standard addressing protocol in business letters*

10 Using visual aids

The most common visual aid used in business communications is the Microsoft PowerPoint presentation. It is typically delivered through a projector on to a screen or through hard-copy handouts. Microsoft PowerPoint is particularly prevalent in professional service industries such as investment banking and consulting. Usually, you can take advantage of specialist people or personal assistants to handle the actual production of presentations. You need to judge whether your job calls for proficiency in using PowerPoint. However, be prepared to design and use presentations as a medium of communication. For example, many first-rungers have to perform at least some analysis and, when discussing any data set, using charts is so much more effective than showing raw data or even tabulated data. We will not discuss how to use PowerPoint because the subject is too vast and worthy of separate study. Any decent bookshop should have a number of books on how to use the program efficiently. Your company may have books and/or tutors available too. On the subject of how to design PowerPoint-type presentations effectively, I recommend two books written by Gene Zelazny: *Say It with Presentations* and *Say It with Charts*, both published by McGraw-Hill. These are excellent books, which show you how to present data, concepts, project plans etc graphically and how to structure your presentations.

Flip charts (and increasingly their technologically more advanced cousins, electronic whiteboards) are probably the next most ubiquitous form of visual aid and are particularly useful in small to medium-size meetings. The key thing to realize is that whoever controls the flip chart has significant control over the meeting, without necessarily being seen to run the meeting. Stepping up to the flip chart is thus a good opportunity for a first-runger to contribute to the meeting and can be done without overstepping your bounds if you position your role as a facilitator rather than as a chairperson.

Three ways to use a flip chart effectively are:

■ **To set the agenda.** An alternative and very effective approach to bringing printed agendas to a meeting is to kick off the meeting by writing up the agenda on a flip chart or whiteboard. This approach has the advantage of being interactive – you can solicit input from other participants to change or add to the agenda as necessary.

■ **To capture 'to-dos'.** Most meetings generate actions that some or all of the meeting participants need to execute. A flip chart or whiteboard is an effective means of capturing all the actions agreed during the course of the meeting. Make sure, when writing 'to-dos', that you also write up who is responsible for which action and, if required, set deadlines. You need people to be responsible for delivering and you will only achieve this by assigning clear accountabilities.

■ **To summarize next steps.** In addition to writing up 'to-dos' during the course of the meeting, use the flip chart or whiteboard to conclude by writing up the next steps. Next steps frequently overlap with 'to-dos' but they may include additional things such as when the meeting participants will reconvene.

Tailoring your personal communication strategy

With so many ways to communicate, figuring out your optimal personal communication strategy can be confusing. Should I send a group e-mail or a group voicemail? Should I set up a meeting or a conference call? How often should I communicate and when? What should I communicate? However, with a little effort, it is not so difficult to hit the mark. Here are three principles you should follow.

1 Adopt your organization's communication culture

The first thing you need to under-stand to target your personal communication strategy is your organization's communication culture – what forms of communi-cation your organization expects you to use. Some firms like to use

The first thing you need to under-stand to target your personal communication strategy is your organization's communication culture.

voicemail, some have an e-mail culture, while others use both. Some organizations make decisions using a consensus approach and therefore tend to have many face-to-face meetings or conference calls.

Frank Gerard joined a small hedge fund after graduating from Harvard Business School in 2001. On his first day, he turned to the colleague sitting next to him and asked him a question. He received a fairly terse reply but thought nothing of it. A couple of minutes later, he received an e-mail from the same colleague informing him that the primary mode of communication in the office was e-mail and that in future he would prefer it if Frank would ask any questions that he might have via the e-mail system.

Procter & Gamble has a memo culture. Luis Costa worked at Procter & Gamble for four years and recalls that most communication was conducted via memos, whether it was about arriving at a decision, sharing information or planning projects.

Goldman Sachs is well known for its voicemail culture. George Malone, who joined the Goldman Sachs New York office after college, recalls having to undergo a full day of voicemail training during his induction programme, where he was taught both the technical side of voicemailing – how to dial into the system, receive and send messages – and the best practices for leaving messages. George recalls that everyone checked voicemail at least once every hour including at weekends. Technology has now progressed to the point where you can programme voicemail to call your mobile phone when it receives new messages, making life a little easier.

Sometimes, organizations are so decentralized that no single communi-cation culture exists. You therefore have to evaluate the communication culture of each specific division or country. Some executives were on graduate programmes and rotated through a number of divisions and countries. Some of these executives found that their company relied on a mix of one-to-one interactions, meetings, voicemail and e-mail, but different divisions had their own preferences; one might have a dominant voicemail culture, another might prefer e-mail while a third would favour face-to-face meetings.

You will not go far wrong if you learn to recognize and adopt your organization's culture. Furthermore, in an individual situation, if you have no other information for deciding how to communicate, your organization's communication culture should be the basis for your default choice.

2 Ask for guidance

In many cases, the communication culture is not so obvious either at the organizational level or within different divisions or geographies. Even when the communication culture is clear, sometimes different bosses and colleagues like doing things their own way – every organization has its mavericks. The best way to make sure your personal communication strategy with specific individuals or groups is effective is simply to ask for guidance.

> The best way to make sure your personal communication strategy with specific individuals or groups is effective is simply to ask for guidance.

Jake Hammond learned the hard way that there is no 'one-size-fits-all' approach to communication. On his first project at a major management consulting firm, the director leading the project took Jake aside after a few weeks. The director told him that he did not feel he was being 'kept in the loop' enough and explicitly requested that Jake send daily voicemail updates from his work stream. Jake, as required, responded by sending a daily voicemail to the director. On his next project, Jake had a different director. Jake, trying to impress this new director by 'keeping him in the loop', diligently updated the director with multiple e-mails throughout the day. However, unfortunately for Jake, this director preferred less frequent contact and more summarized communication than the fine detail Jake had learned to provide on his previous project. On this occasion, the director told Jake's manager that, although Jake was otherwise doing a stellar job on the project, he was getting a bit frustrated at being 'bombarded' with Jake's e-mails.

Jake learned from that point to ask his directors and other team members how best to communicate with them by asking for explicit guidance on the form, frequency and content of their preferred communication.

3 Use common sense

Asking is the surest way to getting your communication strategy right, but sometimes it is not possible to ask. In these cases, you should ensure that you default to your organization's communication culture and apply some basic common-sense principles when it comes to communicating to a broader community of colleagues and clients.

Use the most personal form of communication

Frank Gerard's hedge fund example aside, where possible, speaking to someone face to face is better than the phone or voicemail, and using the phone is better than e-mailing. Similarly, a meeting is preferable to a conference call, and a conference call is usually better than a group discussion via e-mail.

> Speaking to someone face to face is better than the phone or voicemail, and using the phone is better than e-mailing.

Three broad reasons exist for this order of priority. First, communication is a two-way process and in order to communicate well you need to be able to read and respond to your counterpart. Face-to-face interaction is superior to a phone call because you can interpret eye contact and read body language. Similarly, a phone call is preferable to an e-mail, as you read and respond to voice intonations. Second, as we cover later in the book, succeeding on the first rung requires a strong network, mentors and political savvy. All three are developed through relationship building, and using the most personal form of communication is most aligned with relationship building. Third, a ringing phone or new e-mails are often a disturbance to concentration. Such interactions automatically start off on the wrong foot, and in some cases they never recover. While a face-to-face interaction is no less a disturbance, people tend to be more receptive to someone who is present in person. You will find people will actually appreciate your effort in coming to speak to them face to face and they will also be far more cooperative.

Tailor your communication approach for the audience

While it is always best to try to personalize your communication, often because of various constraints it does not make sense to have face-to-face meetings or even phone calls. In such situations, e-mail and voicemail are very flexible because you can send them at your convenience and they can be read or listened to when convenient for the recipient(s). Decide whether it is a better use of your time to share information personally or to use group dissemination.

To use an extreme example, when Jeremy Smith was working in the US marketing department of SmithKline Beecham, he had to send marketing updates to literally hundreds of salespeople who were out on the road across the country. It would have been ludicrous to try to personalize communication in this case. Instead, he used to send a single voicemail copied to the salespeople with the marketing updates.

Sometimes, you need to communicate with people whose schedule makes them unavailable – they may be stuck in meetings all day, travelling or in a different time zone. Voicemail or e-mail is ideal in these situations.

Use written communication when that is best

Use written communication, ie e-mail or memos, when:

- **You need to share detailed information.** Spoken communication becomes hard to follow when you have much information to share. An e-mail or a memo is easier to follow than a long telephone conversation or a large voicemail. When should you choose a memo over an e-mail? If you are sharing something in a very formal capacity, or where there are important mathematical figures to relate, for example, use a memo.

> While face-to-face and phone conversations are more personal than written communication, sometimes you need to have things in written form so that a record exists.

- **You need to make a record.** While face-to-face and phone conversations are more personal than written communication, sometimes you need to have things in written form so that a record exists. Records are important when you need to provide a reference for people. As we discussed in Chapter 3, first-rungers should be like a library resource and have information relating to anything they have worked on filed and stored for easy reference.

■ **You want to create an audit trail.** On some occasions, you may want to keep a record to provide an audit trail. Some executives like to have an audit trail, as it enables them to protect themselves from being blamed for not having communicated or followed up on something. For example, Rachel Lynn, who works at a technology company, will sometimes forward an old e-mail request as a reminder to someone who has not yet responded to a request. Other executives find this approach too aggressive and prefer to chase up using other means.

Combine different forms of communication to cover all bases

Sometimes it makes sense to use more than one communication channel. For example, in my job, when I had to share some detailed information, I would often send an e-mail but, if I knew that the recipient of an e-mail was travelling and might not be checking e-mails unless prompted, I would also leave a voicemail to let the recipient know to expect the e-mail.

In a nutshell – How to learn business communication skills 2

■ When speaking formally one to one:

- always have an agenda prepared;

- warm up with pleasantries;

- establish the time-frame and stick to it;

- use time checks;

- conclude with a summary of agreed actions and next steps.

■ When speaking one to one informally, keep your guard up.

■ If you are running a meeting, take charge.

■ Refer to other people in a meeting by name and build on their comments.

■ Make sure you use a variety of sources on public speaking, and practise through public speaking organizations.

■ When speaking over the telephone, have a professional greeting prepared.

■ When speaking into voicemail, prepare a rough script and repeat your name and contact details.

■ When speaking on conference calls, make sure you know how to set up and run the conference call technology.

■ When writing e-mails, categorize and order recipients to prevent stepping on sensitive egos.

■ Be careful on the 'Reply' and 'Reply All' buttons to avoid sending embarrassing e-mails to large groups.

■ Zip large attachments and send multiple attachments separately to avoid jamming up people's e-mail systems.

- ■ Respond to e-mails rapidly to impress if you can.

- ■ Do not forward jokes by e-mail.

- ■ Treat e-mails like any other professional written work and polish them.

- ■ When writing memos, stick to one page or at least provide a one-page summary.

- ■ When writing business letters:

  - focus on logical structure not visual structure;

  - write in the first person plural, as you are also representing your colleagues;

  - refer to companies as though they were individuals, because legally they are treated equivalently;

  - use formal company stationery;

  - do not forget the recipient's name, title, address and the date;

  - get someone senior to review your letters.

- ■ Make sure you read a variety of sources on using visual aids.

- ■ Use flip charts to set the agenda, capture 'to-dos' and summarize the next steps.

- ■ Establish your personal communication strategy.

Become a great project and people manager

One of the most surprising lessons from writing this book came from an apparent contradiction between the research survey results and the interview findings. The survey showed that not one executive saw managing as an important skill for first-rungers. Surprisingly, when I interviewed executives about what is required to be successful on the first rung, management skills frequently came up as very important, even more so when extended to include upward management and project management.

What explains this anomaly? The survey result certainly seems like the more intuitive result since a first-runger is at the bottom of the career ladder and so has no one below to manage. However,

> When I interviewed executives about what is required to be successful on the first rung, management skills frequently came up as very important.

the reality is that you do have to learn how to manage from day one. The reason why executives highlighted management skills in their interviews and not in the survey is because when they filled out the survey they did not view their first jobs as having any official managerial responsibilities, but when probed they realized that they did have to exercise management skills with others frequently in an unofficial capacity.

When most people think of managing, they naturally think of managing other people. However, particularly for first-rungers, learning how to manage projects is critical. Project management skills are an essential part of the all-round first-runger toolkit and, while they draw on a wide range of intrinsic capabilities such as organizational, people and functional skills, there is a set of principles that the best project managers closely observe and from which you can usefully learn.

Learning how to manage people is difficult for all; executives who assume official management responsibilities have to step up their skill set and capabilities to become effective managers. As a first-runger, however, your challenge is particularly difficult, given that you have to manage unofficially and that you are new and inexperienced by definition.

I recall one instance from my investment banking days when a second-year analyst had to work for the first time with a relatively new associate from Harvard Business School on a marketing pitch that required an 'all-nighter'. The analyst had done numerous such pitches before compared with the new associate. Consequently, despite the analyst's junior position to the associate, the managing director indicated that the analyst was to be held personally responsible for ensuring a high-quality marketing pitch. In other words, he was placed in the position of having to manage completely both the piece of work and the associate. The analyst found it difficult because the new associate was much older, generally more experienced (from work prior to business school), had come from a top-flight business school and was not expecting to have to 'support' someone so junior. Although the analyst and the associate produced a good marketing pitch, the analyst did not handle the associate well. The analyst was arrogant and domineering, even to the point of making sure that the associate was the one who stayed all night while he went home and returned fresh in the morning to proof and 'quality-control' the document. The consequence was that the associate developed a dislike for the analyst, and when the associate was promoted to vice-president a couple of years later he made life generally difficult for the analyst.

Furthermore, the lessons of those executives interviewed who have successfully transitioned from the first rung to the middle rung suggest that the best time to learn how to manage is well before you assume official management responsibility. Vincent York, of a major US consulting firm, recalls, for example, that his first project as an official manager was the hardest and by far the most stressful of all projects he undertook as a consultant. Vincent had been an investment banker for two years at Morgan Stanley; he had spent two years at Stanford Business School; and then he had gained two years of experience as a consultant before he was promoted to an official managerial role. Even with six years of experience, the managerial component of his new role nearly became Vincent's undoing, because he underestimated how much time he had to spend on the people side of the job, having been used to delivering on his own work with little need for supervision from his own manager. Vincent ultimately became an excellent manager, but he would have preferred to have been better equipped before his management skills were thrust into the spotlight.

One particular aspect of managing people, managing upwards, deserves extra-special attention. As a first-runger, you typically have a long line of managers above you, whose responsibilities include managing you either directly or indirectly: they are your bosses. Obviously your bosses exert considerable influence over your career trajectory and also your day-to-day experience. If you want to succeed and if you want your daily experience to be as rewarding as possible you need to manage your bosses.

This chapter, therefore, focuses on these three aspects of managing:

■ managing projects smoothly;
■ managing people for first-rungers;
■ managing upwards.

Managing projects smoothly

Beyond research, analysis and developing communication materials, the rest of a first-rung job centres on projects. Usually projects will include some or all of research, analysis and document-related tasks, but these tasks are merely inputs to achieve a larger, project-orientated goal. While you need to perform each task to high standards, ultimately you must ensure that you meet the goals of the project.

Your ability to manage projects, to 'execute' effectively, is critical

> Your ability to manage projects, to 'execute' effectively, is critical because it is the one where most first-rungers fail.

because it is the one where most first-rungers fail, precisely because it requires that they leverage a broad set of skills to a high standard.

Adopt the following principles to excel at project management and execution.

Take ownership

When you receive an individual task, such as to prepare a memo, you know that you are responsible and that you alone will be held accountable for its accuracy and quality. You take ownership and you are driven to produce high-quality output.

In a project setting, a team of people are usually responsible for the project outcome. While a project manager exists to ensure the team meets the project objectives successfully, projects frequently suffer because team members do not make themselves sufficiently accountable for the whole project; they focus only on their discrete tasks and work streams. Do not be like these team members. Make yourself personally responsible for the outcome of the project. Take ownership. This does not mean that you have to compete with the project manager. David Bruce of Aramark describes taking ownership as a state of mind where your focus shifts from completing assigned tasks to looking to contribute effectively wherever you can to the project's success.

Luis Costa of Procter & Gamble demonstrated taking ownership by closely monitoring a project's progress and noticing if any piece of work fell behind schedule. He not only highlighted any issues to his boss, but he found time around his own assigned tasks to get the relevant pieces of work back on track.

Jack Reardon of American Medical Security calls it being a team player. True team players, he explains, are not focused on their performance, but on the collective performance of their team.

Manage the process

The big difference between project management and discrete tasks such as writing a memo is that process is much more important

> Process is much more important in a project than in an individual task.

in a project than in an individual task. You have to consider not only what you are trying to achieve but also the best way to go about achieving it. A project typically involves the collaboration of a broad group of people, often including people outside the direct project team and a set of often simultaneous, overlapping and interlinked tasks.

When Jake Hammond of a major consulting firm was conducting an interview programme, he realized that there were several constituent steps involved in the process. The process he followed included the following tasks:

■ Obtain the names and numbers of potential interview candidates from the client.
■ Supplement client-provided interview candidates with cold-call names.
■ Establish the availability of senior colleagues to conduct the interviews.
■ Call the interview candidates and schedule the interviews.
■ Provide senior colleagues with preparatory materials on the interviewees.
■ Conduct the interviews with senior colleagues.
■ Write up the interview notes.

The key to Jake completing the project, which required 50 interviews in eight weeks successfully and on time, was not following this process sequence in strict order, even if it appeared a logical progression, but thinking ahead and figuring out what had to happen and when.

Pay attention to 'lead and cycle times' – how long it takes to prepare (lead time) and complete (cycle time) each task in a process – to deliver on time, particularly where your ability to action other tasks is contingent on delivery.

The main reason most projects are delayed is because project teams underappreciate lead and cycle times and contingencies or interlinkages within a process.

In the interview programme example, Jake realized that the preparatory materials on the interviewees took a week to complete because the research department required two days' notice (lead time) and three days to complete the task (cycle time), so he made sure that he notified the research department to work on the preparatory materials even before he scheduled any interviews. As the interviews became scheduled, he prioritized which interview materials the researchers had to prepare so that earlier interviews were prioritized over later interviews. He checked in and followed up to make sure that the research department was on top of everything. Less aware executives would only have thought about producing interview preparatory materials once the interviews were scheduled and only then would they have realized that they had left insufficient time.

Follow up firmly but politely

One of the more difficult aspects of effective project management is following up on people who have agreed or are supposed to contribute to some piece of work. As you will soon find from your own day-to-day activities, you are frequently interrupted with random requests from all kinds of people. Even the most organized people let some things slip and need reminding. You need to follow up with these people and get them to complete their tasks on time in order to keep the project on track.

When Kirk Williams of Chrysler needs to follow up with someone, he starts out by dropping an e-mail or making a call as a polite reminder, and assumes that the task has slipped the person's mind. He allows them to save face by not being accusatory. Usually, a polite reminder is all that it takes to jog someone into action. If this does not work, Kirk makes sure he speaks to the person and, remaining polite, asks the person to provide a deadline by which he can expect to receive the completed work. He does this by asking: 'When do you expect to have completed the end-product?' This way he gets the person to sign up to meeting a deadline.

If the request is unimportant or can be completed some other way without too much pain and if someone is not responsive, it may make sense to circumvent the person. If possible, it is always better to avoid a nasty confrontation or falling out. If, however, this person is essential to a project or if circumventing him or her will cause undue pain and time loss, then you need to find a way to get the person to deliver.

Colin Hobart of Reuters is one of many executives who follow a clear path of escalation if the request is important and cannot be circumvented. He also initially gives the other person the benefit of the doubt and tries to be as casual as possible with his reminder, which is usually via e-mail or voicemail. If that does not work, he remains casual and keeps a sense of humour, but will visit the person or call and speak to him or her directly, while maintaining a light touch. He will try that a couple of times and, if that does not work, he sends the person an e-mail, copying his superiors. Finally, he will send an e-mail, copying both his superiors and the other person's superiors – effectively paving the way for senior intervention in the matter. This should absolutely be a last resort, as it conflicts with the 'no-enemy policy' that we discuss in Chapter 9.

One thing I have found effective in these circumstances is to ask how I can help the person get the work done on time. You have to be careful that he or she does not unload the task on to you, but you make it harder for the person to find excuses.

Be flexible

In line with taking ownership and being a team player is a willingness to help regardless of the type of task. Be flexible and do not consider any tasks beneath you even if they fall outside of the standard information, analysis and document task-related categories described here. If a task needs to be done and you can help, then help. Not only will you contribute where needed, but you will earn respect for not having a superior attitude.

Dan Barker of US Robotics believes that too many first-rungers are unwilling to get involved in menial tasks. They walk into their new jobs, he says, with a degree, expecting to do an intellectual job, and they turn their noses up at anything that requires them to 'roll up their sleeves'. Dan says his willingness to get involved in menial tasks, such as helping the fork-lift truck driver to ensure a shipment went out on time, sometimes made more difference to a project's success than sitting in his office writing the most perfect memo or performing the most insightful analysis.

Jeff Callahan of Schroders agrees. He is one of only a few executives who will help the people in the print room to print and bind important meeting documents. Other executives, he explains, would never consider such an activity a valid use of their time. Jeff also builds strong relationships this way – who do you think the print room people help first when Jeff is under pressure?

Use a project plan

All projects start with a project plan. The key dimensions of a project plan are a time line, key actions and accountabilities for those actions, and milestones (critical progress points in the project time-frame). Figure

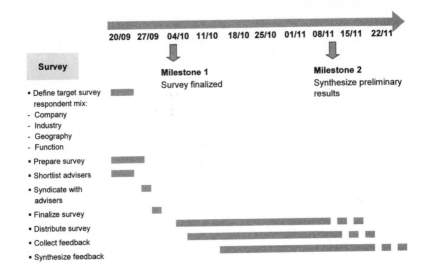

Figure 6.1 *Example project plan*

6.1 is part of the project plan I used to prepare for writing this book. This project plan is called a 'Gantt chart' and details the time-frame, actions and milestones for conducting the broad survey of high-flying executives. In this example, the project plan excludes accountabilities because I knew that *I* was responsible for all of these actions!

Many companies have their preferred style of project plan, whether it is using a standard project management programme or adopting a specific output format. Seek examples of well-regarded project plans that have been used previously, copy the style and include the same elements in your project plan.

Delegate

The secret to managing effectively and optimizing your own productivity is learning how to delegate. Because you are a first-

> The secret to managing effectively and optimizing your own productivity is learning how to delegate.

runger, your ability to delegate is limited. However, you need to get used to the idea that, in your professional role of managing a project or part of a project, you are a marshal of resources. You need to find the right people to do the right task and you need to get them to contribute appropriately.

The first mistake first-rungers make is being too timid. They are afraid to ask people to do work even when it is appropriate to do so. There is no need. Most people are professional and they will recognize why they have to do something and will ensure that they meet a deadline. They will further recognize that you are doing your job when you ask them.

In cases where it is not so clear cut that something is another person's responsibility, you can still be direct and ask, but you need to be savvier. One trick some executives mentioned is to delegate but delegate indirectly. Ultimately all your projects are endorsed by someone much more senior than you are. Borrow authority from the senior people involved in the project, and make people feel as though they are helping out the senior people rather than you. You can do this by saying that you are working for your boss on a project and that the boss's boss would like further help on the project.

Syndicate

Syndication is sharing and disseminating partially or near-completed work with a 'syndicate' of people who can provide feedback, comments and input to your work. In the same way that delegating is important in optimizing your productivity, so syndication is important in ensuring that your work is high-quality. Furthermore, the process of involving people in the process helps secure 'buy-in' to any work that you do. Ensuring that people 'buy in' to the output or direction of a piece of work is as important as, if not more important than, the quality and correctness of the work itself. The best analysis in the world is of no help if no one believes in, or acts on, it.

Typically, you should syndicate with two types of people: 1) 'stakeholders': anyone who is directly involved in or affected by the work, such as project team members, project managers and project affiliates; 2) 'experts': colleagues who most people in the organization recognize are authorities within the areas of their expertise. For both of these types, pay attention to confidentiality – only syndicate to people you know are allowed to be privy to the work.

One executive worked on a project to launch a product line extension because customer feedback strongly indicated a big market would develop. In order to get management approval for the line extension, this executive had to submit a proposal signed by a recognized list of 'stakeholders', which included senior executives from the finance, research and development, legal, regulatory and sales divisions. The executive realized that the only way that these other executives would sign the proposal was if they had been involved in the process. She made sure that she syndicated the proposal multiple times throughout its preparation, collecting comments and feedback before finalizing a proposal that everyone supported and was willing to adopt.

Carl Moran of General Electric learned early on from his manager who the experts were in his group, and whenever he worked on something that touched their area of expertise he tried where possible to syndicate his work with them. When he submitted his work, not only was it higher-quality, but he was able to support it much more credibly by referring to the well-known experts who had seen it and added their input.

Keep people in the loop

One of the most important things I have learned in my career, and one that many of the executives whom I have interviewed echo, is to 'keep people in the loop', to keep them abreast of what is going

> One of the most important things I have learned in my career, and one that many of the executives whom I have interviewed echo, is to 'keep people in the loop'.

on in the project – its status, key developments etc – and involved where necessary during the process. As with syndication, any 'stakeholder' should be kept in the loop and, to the extent that colleagues, such as 'experts', have contributed to a piece of work, as a matter of professional courtesy you should keep them in the loop too.

George Malone of Goldman Sachs emphasizes the need to keep people up to date on progress, because he believes that many bosses assume nothing is being done in the absence of any information.

Lawrence Fowler of GlaxoSmithKline adds that keeping people in the loop is important not only to prevent your bosses from thinking you are doing nothing, but to get them comfortable that you are going to deliver on time and with high-quality output. It is not good enough, throughout the process of completing a piece of work, that you know that you are going to deliver on time and that your output is going to be high-quality; your superiors need to feel this way too.

Managing people for first-rungers

There are two types of authority that empower executives to manage or lead – informal authority and formal, or positional, authority. Formal authority arises from one's position in a hierarchical organizational structure – a captain in an army has formal authority over a sergeant purely because of rank. Informal authority is built on achievement, experience and respect – an experienced sergeant may have more informal authority over the platoon soldiers than a brand-new, inexperienced captain. Every organization has individuals who, despite possessing impressive titles and seemingly senior positions, lack any meaningful influence because, ultimately, they command little respect. The only sway that such individuals have is through 'pulling rank'. Conversely, you will also encounter individuals who, although lacking impressive titles and senior positions, hold significant influence because they possess informal authority.

As a first-runger, you rarely have any formal authority. Even if you quickly assume an official management role, do not be fooled into thinking that you have any meaningful authority, because the reality is that you are new and inexperienced and have yet to earn the respect that accompanies informal authority.

Although you can expect to have no official managerial responsibility, you need to realize that you still have to manage people. Every interaction that you have with people, particularly if it involves working with them or getting them to do a piece of work, requires that you manage them. So with neither real formal authority nor informal authority, how is a first-runger to stand a chance of managing anyone – even in an unofficial capacity?

> With neither real formal authority nor informal authority, how is a first-runger to stand a chance of managing anyone – even in an unofficial capacity?

In Chapter 1, we talked about the importance of being genuinely humble – as Luke Patella of Bain & Company puts it, 'You must leave the ego at home.' When it comes to managing, particularly as a first-runger, humility and lack of ego are critically important. If someone suspects that you are on a power trip, they will resent your managing them and create problems for you.

This does not mean that you have to be timid and afraid of stepping on toes, but it does mean that your approach has to be different to that of a manager with real authority. The secret is a 'quiet management' approach. With a quiet management approach, those whom you are managing do not feel as though they are

> The secret is a 'quiet management' approach. With a quiet management approach, those whom you are managing do not feel as though they are being managed.

being managed. This is important to appreciate, because the last thing executives like is the feeling that someone less senior or at the same level is trying to manage them. It is important to understand that the quiet management approach is not a single style; everyone has his or her own way of interacting with people. The point is that, for a first-runger, the degrees of freedom to manage people are limited, and a quiet management approach recognizes these limitations. Within the degrees of freedom available, you should feel comfortable with whichever style is most natural to you. The investment banking associate in the story at the start of this chapter appreciated that the analyst knew more about putting together a marketing pitch than he did, but he did not appreciate the analyst being autocratic and didactic in his style. He would have much preferred someone to manage him more subtly. The following are the key principles of a first-runger quiet management approach.

Observe first-rung management boundaries

An important part of being successful as a first-runger comes down to understanding your limitations and the organizational boundaries in which you have to operate. Nowhere is this more important than when you have to manage people in an unofficial capacity. Figure 6.2 breaks down the core responsibilities that a fully fledged manager has to undertake, details those that are strictly off limits for a first-runger, and also details important constraints on those that are, at least partly, appropriate. In other words, it describes the available degrees of freedom to manage for a first-runger.

Of course, if you are one of the rare first-rungers who have official management duties, then your boundaries may be a little broader, but you would still be wise to observe a quiet management approach if you do not wish to ruffle too many feathers.

Core manager responsibilities	First-rung quiet approach
Setting objectives/direction	✓ – only with consensus
Driving work plans	✓ – only with consensus
Monitoring progress	✓ – follow up firmly but politely*
Ensuring quality control	✓ – first-runger is always first quality filter
Coaching/feedback	✗ – except for genuine appreciation/gratitude
Evaluation/review	✗ – do not be tempted

*See 'Managing projects smoothly'

Figure 6.2   *Core manager responsibilities versus the first-rung quiet approach*

Be consensus-driven, not autocratic

Two contrasting types of management approaches are 'consensus-driven' and 'autocratic'. Consensus-driven managers involve their colleagues in the decision-making process. They try to secure agreement through discussion and get everybody on board with what needs to be done. Autocratic managers, on the other hand, independently decide a course of action and direct people to follow their decisions whether the people are in agreement or not.

Many first-rungers fall into the trap of thinking that managers have to be autocratic. Brian Murphy of Ericsson, for example, believes that many first-rungers

> Many first-rungers fall into the trap of thinking that managers have to be autocratic.

are either too afraid to try to manage someone or are too demanding. There are certainly times when an autocratic leader is most effective. For example, in a crisis or high-pressure situation, someone must take charge and call the shots. In reality, however, good managers are able to function anywhere along the spectrum between these two extremes, depending on the situation. For a first-runger, the consensus-driven approach is usually the more effective option.

With a consensus-driven approach, first-rungers can avoid people feeling that they are actually being managed. James Edwards of Novartis argues that a first-runger needs to think more about 'facilitating' than 'managing' or 'directing'. Facilitation is an excellent way to think about managing in general, as it encourages you to adopt an approach that finds ways to make people willingly choose to do those things you need them to do. Kirk Williams of Chrysler agrees with this notion and believes that, if you can make other people feel as though they are deciding what they have to do instead of you deciding for them, then they will be more willing to do it and will also be more committed to doing it better. Harriet Giggs of PricewaterhouseCoopers puts it another way; she says that managing people is less about persuading and more about securing buy-in for what needs to be done.

Always ask, never tell

Even if you successfully employ a consensus-driven approach where everyone agrees on what work needs to be done, you often still have to go through the exercise of deciding and agreeing who is going to do the work. This should not be unduly arduous, but it is an important aspect of quiet management to ask people to do a piece of work instead of telling them. The difference in psychology between asking and telling is enormous. As Jack Reardon of American Medical Security puts it: 'Nobody likes "to be told" what to do', and that is particularly true when it is a first-runger who is doing the telling. Asking, on the other hand, allows people to feel that they have a say, because they have the implicit option of saying no. By saying something like: 'Anne, would you be able to work on this?', you make your request without placing undue pressure on anyone. Of course, people can also refuse to 'do what they are told', but this requires a much greater degree of confrontation, and you would do well to avoid facilitating such a reaction.

Get the other person to define crystal-clear deliverables and time line

Once you have managed to get someone to agree that a task needs to be completed and to take on the responsibility, you need to be sure that the person understands exactly what he or she needs to deliver and by when. This can be a tricky exercise, because the other person can feel micromanaged. Nevertheless, it is critical that everyone is clear on deliverables and time line if a project or piece of work is to come together smoothly. You will be surprised at how different people's views can be on the specific steps that need to be taken, even after apparently clear consensus. Furthermore, many people will say that they know what they have to do, not because they actually know, but in the hope that they can work it out afterwards.

> It is critical that everyone is clear on deliverables and time lines if a project or piece of work is to come together smoothly.

I recently learned this lesson with a team I was managing. A team meeting concluded with the team discussing at length next steps for a project and the key analyses and research the team had to conduct. In my own head, I had a crystal-clear picture of what each team member needed to do and thought that, because it was obvious to me, it must be obvious to my team. I was wrong. It was actually my team that forced me to articulate the next steps on a whiteboard to make sure that we all understood them in the same way and, of course, only after the exercise did we actually align our understanding. You will not always be able to rely on your colleagues to create such mutual understanding, so it is up to you.

How do you actually get someone to agree deliverables and time line without micromanaging? The answer is to focus on the time line first. If you focus on the deliverables first, it will feel repetitive to the other person, who may think that he or she has already gained a clear picture from the previous discussions. However, the exact time line is something that you will probably not yet have discussed or agreed explicitly. The benefit of focusing on the time line first is that it simultaneously forces a mutual understanding of the deliverables, because they are the critical input into the time line.

In terms of conducting the discussion, James Wentworth of Bain & Company advocates giving the other person the lead. He summarizes the deliverables as inputs into the time line and then asks the other person to set the time line and specific deadlines. This is a great approach, as it allows James to recap the deliverables in a way that is helpful while making the other person feel that he or she is in charge of the schedule. Typically, people come back with time lines that are reasonable, and the discussion ends there. If you need to 'negotiate' the time line, the approach I prefer is simply to ask if there is any way that the other person could meet an earlier time line, and explain why this would be preferable in terms of the project (but not in terms of how it would make your own life easier).

If reaching an agreement on a time line is proving difficult, the approach that Vincent York of Morgan Stanley takes is to ask the other person what it would take for him or her to meet the deadline. This is a good question, because it forces orientation towards solutions instead of problems.

The final thing you can do to be sure that everyone shares a common understanding is to write a short e-mail summarizing the deliverables and time line. Getting the deliverables and time line down in written and recorded form is the ultimate in ensuring alignment, but be careful that you do so in a manner that is helpful rather than micromanaging. This is a matter of positioning and needs little more than something like the following for an introduction: 'Thanks for your help on this. Thought it might be helpful to summarize the discussion in an e-mail...'

Show gratitude and appreciation

When people have done a piece of work for you, even though it may be part of their job and they 'have' to do it, a show of gratitude and, if merited, genuine appreciation for the quality of their output is the final aspect of quiet management.

Harriet Giggs of PricewaterhouseCoopers argues that, by showing gratitude and appreciation, you reinforce the mindset that someone is helping you rather than being managed by you. Alan Wilson of Constellation Energy agrees and believes that, if you show people gratitude and appreciation, they are more likely to want to help you in the future because they know that you recognize their efforts.

> By showing gratitude and appreciation, you reinforce the mindset that someone is helping you rather than being managed by you.

Managing upwards

One of the most forgotten aspects of management, which ironically increases in importance over the course of a career, is managing upwards. Obviously, the most important dimensions of

> One of the most forgotten aspects of management, which ironically increases in importance over the course of a career, is managing upwards.

managing upward centre on having a good attitude and doing good work, but the cleverest first-rungers learn very early on that managing their bosses is critical to success. The following are the key general principles to observe to ensure that your relationship with your boss is as effective as possible. These principles apply to all types of bosses, but you will also need to tailor your approach to different types of managers.

Understand your boss

One of the important dimensions of attitude that we covered in Chapter 1 was proactivity. Recall the exercise we went through, as recommended by Mary Peters of Microsoft, of mentally putting yourself in the position of your boss. While the focus was to appreciate how much bosses value genuine proactivity, in reality this exercise is essential to understanding bosses on a broader level, what drives them and what they value. Brian Murphy of Ericsson agrees and argues that too few first-rungers take the time to 'put themselves in other people's shoes'. If you can understand your bosses, you are halfway to learning how to manage them.

Melissa Castle of Honeywell is a strong believer in getting to know about people beyond their role as colleagues or bosses. She argues that, if you know more about your boss than what you see in the office, you are in a much better place to understand him or her. For example, if you know that your boss has a newborn baby, you can prepare yourself for a shift in the boss's priorities and a little moodiness caused by lack of sleep.

Mark Jackson of Dell believes that another important way to understand your boss is 'to get to know their priorities, and what motivations lie underneath their priorities'. At the outset of a piece of work with a new boss, Mark ensures that he 'presses' his boss 'for their priorities'. He is then able to make sure his effort is in line with these priorities.

Instil confidence

While every boss is different, there are some common truths that you should recognize to manage upwards effectively. The first of these common truths is that

Bosses need to feel confident that you will deliver. You must consciously and actively make it your responsibility to instil this confidence.

bosses need to feel confident that you will deliver. You must consciously and actively make it your responsibility to instil this confidence. Of course, over time your consistent performance is the surest way to instil confidence but, even if you are a consistent high performer, bosses will still have bouts of uncertainty, and your ability to lessen their concerns is critical.

One executive recalled a meeting where he had to present some company financial information to a set of that company's managers. In the rehearsal presentation, the team noticed that internal contradictions existed in the numbers. It turned out that these contradictions arose from mistakes in the source data, and so no one was at fault. The managing director, however, was understandably worried that the presentation would unravel on the back of these questionable numbers. The managing director turned to this executive, and asked him if he was confident he could present with these numbers. The executive looked his managing director directly in the eye and without hesitation said 'Absolutely.' He knew that this was the only acceptable answer. Had he said anything else, the managing director would have been nervous and unhappy. Of course, the executive was left with the task of presenting, but found a way to present successfully and focus on the key messages that did not rely on the contradictions in numbers.

While it is critical to instil confidence in your bosses, do not make the mistake of telling bosses what they want to hear if you know it is unrealistic. While you may successfully instil confidence in the short term, you will utterly shatter confidence over the long term if you do not deliver. Not only will you not have delivered, but you will have lost all credibility. It can take a long time to build confidence, but a very short time to destroy it.

Manage expectations by 'under-promising and over-delivering'

There is an expression that I was taught very early on in my career and one that was mentioned by a number of executives. This expression is 'under-promise, over-deliver'. The principle behind this expression is one of managing expectations. While it is important to instil confidence in your bosses, you need to make sure that you do not over-promise and over-commit. This is a very short-term approach to winning confidence and, again, if you do not meet your promise, you ultimately destroy confidence.

There are two sides to 'under-promise, over-deliver'. The first and initial side is to under-promise. For example, if you are discussing a project with your boss, you would be wise not to elaborate on all the amazing things you are going to do in your analysis and how fancy the output and conclusions are going to be. Instead you should focus on the practical requirements and outputs, and commit to delivering these and nothing more. Do not try to under-promise any further, because then you are promising to under-deliver, and that is no good either.

The second side is the over-delivering. Over-delivering might include running additional analysis, which improves the ability to make a decision, or beating a tough deadline. The point on over-delivering is not to do more than is required for the sake of it, but to do more than is asked or agreed because it is helpful and 'adds value' in the eyes of your boss.

Raise genuine issues early but be sure to provide potential solutions

Bosses hate surprises, especially bad surprises. The reality is that not all things go to plan, and sometimes things go very wrong. You must face the responsibility of raising issues with your boss and raising them early. The central question here is: what constitutes a genuine issue? The answer: any issue that you cannot resolve on your own or within your team.

> Bosses hate surprises, especially bad surprises... You must face the responsibility of raising issues with your boss and raising them early.

I was recently involved in a project where one of my team members appeared disengaged from the problem. He was clearly very talented and capable, but his attention seemed to be elsewhere. In meetings, he would not participate, he arrived late and his general energy levels were low. My boss, I suspected, was aware of the issue but had not said anything to me. After two days of observing the same behaviour, I mentioned the issue to my boss, and suggested that I speak with this particular team member and deal with the situation myself. My boss agreed with this proposal.

Fortunately, the team member was very responsive and upon listening to my perspective, although not delighted to receive the feedback, was grateful for being told early on in the project. He more than proved himself on the project after that conversation. What I achieved was a number of things: I earned the trust of the team member by being up front and straight; I covered myself by making sure that I would not be viewed negatively if he failed; I demonstrated proactivity in dealing with the situation; and I demonstrated team management skills to my own boss by resolving the problem on my own.

Keep your boss in the loop

Bosses like to be kept in the loop on the progress and performance of all your work, not just a specific project. As Lawrence Fowler of GlaxoSmithKline puts it, 'Keep your bosses in the loop. Let them know what you have been doing and where you are heading in your work.' The way that Lawrence did this in practical terms was to set up weekly meetings for 30 minutes with his boss, and he used that time as a formal mechanism to update and inform. Lawrence's boss not only gained confidence that Lawrence was on top of his work but was also able to offer advice and help resolve any issues.

Even if you resolve issues without your boss's intervention, you would be wise to keep your boss informed of those issues that you have faced and resolved. Your boss will appreciate you keeping him or her informed and will also recognize your skills in handling issues independently. On another level, it is a good idea to make your boss aware of issues that you have resolved because issues have a tendency of recurring and you may not always be in a position to resolve the issue the next time. Bosses tend to have a much greater appreciation of the issue if they have been made aware of the general nature of the problem beforehand.

How you keep your boss in the loop is a question of his or her personal preferences. As we discussed in Chapter 5, finding out the best mode of communication by asking for direct guidance is the surest way to hit the mark.

Make your boss's life easier

In Chapter 1, we highlighted the importance of being flexible and helpful. One of the examples used to illustrate this point was of Florence Elias of NBC, who answered the phone and took messages for her boss. Florence was helpful, and flexible in the way she was helpful, because she knew it made her boss's life easier and, in the context of her job, it did not cost her anything to be helpful in these ways.

Make your boss look good

The final common truth is that bosses like to look good. Your bosses have their own bosses and, just as you want to look good in front of your boss, your boss wants to look good in front of his or her boss. What can you do, as Mark Jackson of Dell puts it, 'to make your boss look good', apart from ensuring that you provide all the support he or she could ever ask for and that you deliver top-quality work? The answer is marketing.

Marketing is about controlling perception and, when we talk about making your boss look good, it is about contributing to that perception. Obviously, you should not make random things up, but the more you can extol your boss's virtues and enthuse about your experience of working with him or her, the greater the likelihood of enhancing your boss's reputation. This is not about undeserved flattery; it is about genuinely acknowledging your boss's strengths and the positives of your working experience. Indeed, you will not be flattering your boss directly. The point of making your boss look good is telling others, not your boss, about his or her qualities.

In a nutshell – How to become a great project and people manager

■ Take ownership of the project and make it your responsibility to deliver.

■ Manage the process, not just the output.

■ Follow up firmly but politely to ensure that project deliverables are met on time.

■ Be flexible in your role on the project team.

■ Use a project plan.

■ Delegate to improve your own productivity.

■ Syndicate to stakeholders and experts.

■ Keep people in the loop.

■ Learn the rules of quiet management:

  – Observe first-runger management boundaries.

  – Be consensus-driven, not autocratic.

  – Always ask, never tell.

  – Get the other person to define crystal-clear deliverables and time line.

  – Show gratitude and appreciation to reinforce the mindset that someone is helping you rather than being managed by you.

■ Understand your boss.

■ Manage your boss's expectations by 'under-promising and over-delivering'.

■ Raise genuine issues early but be sure to provide potential solutions.

■ Keep your boss in the loop on what you have been doing and where you intend to focus in the future.

■ Make your boss's life easier by being helpful.

■ Make your boss look good by marketing, as well as delivering for, him or her.

Part 3

Navigate the political organization

7

Build your network

Few disagree that networks are a powerful influence in a career. In Chapter 3, we briefly discussed 'information networks' and 'knowledge networks' and their importance in becoming an excellent research analyst. In fact, the interdependent nature of the business world requires networks to function effectively in all manner of capacities, and your ability to build effective networks is critical.

While most people recognize the importance of networks, many people, both those on the first rung and those further along in their career, do not understand how to build truly effective networks. For some, the very notion of networking lacks dignity, because they believe it is contrived and ultimately self-interested. They prefer not to cheapen themselves by engaging in 'shallow' networking practices. In reality, they do have networks, whether they realize it or not and, while they may not explicitly build large networks, their networks are often very powerful, though small, because they have developed naturally from strong relationships. Others have embraced networking in such an overtly self-interested fashion that, although they believe that they have a wide range of contacts, their networks are often relatively ineffective – no one likes someone who is disingenuous.

> Many people, both those on the first rung and those further along in their career, do not understand how to build truly effective networks.

The executives surveyed for this book recognized the importance of networking in their own first-rung careers. In fact, of things that they wish they had known before starting out in their career, over a third, unprompted, mentioned how to network effectively. They confirm my own experience that the most powerful networks develop from real relationships and remain important throughout an entire career. They also highlighted a critical link with attitude, behaviours and interpersonal skills.

In this chapter we cover the following:

- ■ why networks are important;
- ■ the effective network;
- ■ building deep networks;
- ■ building broad networks.

Why networks are important

Business is about people, and it is a rare organization that does not talk about its people as its most precious resource. The more people you know and the more people who know you and respect you the better. As Chris Moritz of Teligent put it, you need to be 'plugged in'. Being 'plugged in' comes from having effective networks. You need relationships with the people whom you have to work with, whether they are sitting across the desk from you or on the other side of the globe. You need to know those who can help you in your job. You need to learn from people who know more than you do or have greater experience than you. You need to know people who affect your project assignments and have an impact on your evaluations. All these people need to be part of your networks, and you need to spend time cultivating them.

Luis Costa of Procter & Gamble makes the point that networks facilitate your day-to-day job performance because people are naturally more inclined to trust, confide in and cooperate with you if they have a relationship with you than they will someone unfamiliar.

Mark Jackson of Dell believes that the process of developing networks, as well as the networks themselves, helps to develop a deep understanding of the business and the priorities that drive decision making because part of getting to know people in a professional context involves learning about their jobs and roles in the organization.

You will benefit in several ways from broad and deep networks. Many executives interviewed for this book highlighted several if not all of the following benefits.

Career and job opportunities

Naive is the person who thinks that career and job opportunities are solely a function of merit. Merit is, of course, important. As Tom Brent of Disney put it, 'It all starts with your basic performance.' But merit counts for nothing if the right people do not know about it. The reality is that, when managers try to staff a new project or a new job, they tend to rely most often on their colleagues to suggest candidates or they choose someone directly from their own network. If you have a strong network within an organization, many people will know your name, and, assuming that you have performed well, the more people who know, the more likely they are to volunteer you.

Even if you proactively go after a project or a role, the power of your network comes to the fore, as managers tend to vet candidates with their colleagues and, if their colleagues know you, they are more likely to lend their support.

Several executives noted the importance of a good word-of-mouth reputation. David Bruce of Aramark attributes a number of his assignments to the good word-of-mouth reputation that he developed through his network and performance. These assignments were not only within his local office; they were across the entire United States. David's network was truly broad. As he puts it, 'You have to put your name out there. If people are talking about you, it creates opportunities.'

> Several executives noted the importance of a good word-of-mouth reputation.

George Malone of Goldman Sachs, who worked in a small investment group in New York, similarly benefited from a word-of-mouth reputation generated by his network. George was offered a role of greater responsibility and autonomy in Goldman Sachs' London office because he was extremely well regarded for his 'relentless' work ethic and excellent delivery. The managing director in London had heard that George commanded considerable respect from his New York colleagues and from his own team members who had worked with George previously. Consequently, he sought George for a new role in his group.

Power to delegate and syndicate

In Chapter 6, we covered the importance of delegation and syndication in project management.

Recall that delegating requires that you be a 'marshal of resources'. A strong network will enhance your understanding of where those resources exist and increase your connectivity with those resources – both important precursors of delegating. If you know to whom you can delegate and also have a relationship with the person, then it is a matter of how you delegate.

In addition to increasing scope for delegation, a broad network enables you to syndicate more effectively. Recall that there are usually two categories of people to whom you need to syndicate, 'stakeholders' and 'experts'. You should, by definition, syndicate with stakeholders, but the broader and deeper your network, the more access you have to 'experts' and the more likely they are to commit real time to inputting into your work.

In addition to increasing scope for delegation, a broad network enables you to syndicate more effectively.

Access

One of the attractive features of the Harvard MBA is its alumni network. Harvard Business School's alumni run many of the world's most famous organizations, including IBM, General Electric, Cadbury-Schweppes and WPP, and at the time of writing one even sits in the White House. However, while the younger echelons of the alumni network may not include such high-powered members, the alumni network still serves its younger, more junior members very well. Many of Harvard Business School's freshly minted MBAs begin their job search by scanning the *Alumni Directory* for leads in their chosen areas of interest. They set up 'information chats' and find potential leads for opportunities. Many of these MBAs found their current jobs this way.

The *Alumni Directory*, however, is not a set of relationships. Most Harvard Business School graduates tend to have direct relationships only within their own class and maybe within those two classes that sandwich their graduating class (the MBA is a two-year programme), but it does provide access, and access is very important.

Access is the ability to call on someone even if there is no relationship. If the person is willing to talk to you or see you, then you have access to that person. Access comes from links with

Access is the ability to call on someone even if there is no relationship... Access comes from links with institutions but most importantly with people.

institutions but most importantly with people. The Harvard Business School alumni network's link is obviously Harvard Business School. Within your own network, every relationship that you have is a link to everyone that they know.

Lawrence Fowler of GlaxoSmithKline recalls a physician calling him for help on understanding how to market his emerging private practice better. Lawrence was not a marketer, but he knew someone in marketing within his own network and effectively brokered a conversation between the physician and his contact in marketing. The physician had access to the marketing expert through his relationship with Lawrence.

The great thing about networks is that, as you grow your network, assuming you are building a genuine network, your access to all kinds of people and resources grows much faster. There is an exponential effect. If you have a network of real relationships with 100 people and all of those people have their own networks of 100 people, ignoring overlaps you have access to 10,000 people (100 times 100).

Projection of a positive reputation

Word-of-mouth reputation does not only benefit you in the form of career and job opportunities; your evaluations, promotions and even your performance are all linked to your word-of-mouth reputation.

Kirk Williams of Chrysler is an example of someone benefiting during his evaluation from a good word-of-mouth reputation generated by his network. He received the highest bonus in his group because his boss had heard from a number of people that Kirk was a hard worker and great team player.

A good word-of-mouth reputation helps your performance because: more of the best people want to work with you; colleagues are more cooperative with those whom they professionally respect; and people's preconceptions tend to make them cast you in a more favourable light to begin with – people tend to notice supporting rather than contradictory evidence for their preconceptions.

One pharmaceutical first-rung executive found that he was pulled into some of the best departments during his graduate programme rotations. Because his network recognized and spoke of this executive's high standard of performance, managers in other departments expressed specific interest in getting him into their teams on his next rotation.

Learning and development

The information and learning networks that we have discussed are vital to your ability to grow and develop in your role. By building a set of relationships with people who are able to advise you and teach you the ropes, you will vastly improve the speed with which you climb the learning curve.

> By building a set of relationships with people who are able to advise you and teach you the ropes, you will vastly improve the speed with which you climb the learning curve.

For further reading on the power of networking, a good book is *Linked: The new science of networks* by Albert-László Barabási, which expounds in greater depth on a number of the themes that the executives interviewed highlighted and that we cover here.

The effective network

The benefits of effective networks should now be clear. The challenge remains to build them. Not only did over a third of the executives surveyed wish that they had learned the importance of networking and how to network earlier in their career, but most of them felt that even today they were not particularly good at networking per se. Mary Peters of Microsoft, for example, commented: 'I am not someone who goes out and markets myself aggressively to build my network.'

This struck me as somewhat strange because, in actual fact, when Mary and others described their networks it was evident that they had excellent networks, both broad and deep. Anna Lloyd of the Boston Consulting Group believed she did not network at all, although on close inspection she had a very effective network, even if she had not explicitly cultivated it.

How is it that executives with such great networks think they are poor networkers? The reason is that their, and a common, perception of what it means to be a good networker is misaligned with building truly effective networks. When these executives talked about networking, they focused on the ability to make 'cold contacts', such as being able to enter a room full of strangers and walk out with 20 business cards or numbers. Obviously, if you possess this ability, you have an asset. The reality, though, is that few people are truly comfortable in a room full of strangers, and those who believe they are good at canvassing such a room overestimate the strength of the networks they create in this way.

> Few people are truly comfortable in a room full of strangers, and those who believe they are good at canvassing such a room overestimate the strength of the networks they create in this way.

James Edwards of Novartis described this type of network well: 'a set of contacts that potentially provide professional value'. Read that description again – it sounds cold and clinical. If someone spoke to you only because of your 'potential professional value' to him or her, would you feel any real affinity with that person? I doubt it. There are plenty of books that profess to teach you how to develop these kinds of skills, and they have their use up to a point, but what this chapter focuses on is how to build networks consisting of real relationships.

It turns out that many of the executives surveyed explicitly cultivated part of their networks. However, they also recognized that they were constantly in the process of building and developing their networks even if it was not an explicit, premeditated effort. The important common factor is that their networks were based on real relationships – more 'friendships' than 'business contacts'. However, even for the parts of their networks that developed naturally, most executives recognized that they did a number of things that effectively facilitated the building of the network even although they were not consciously trying to network.

> The important common factor is that their networks were based on real relationships – more 'friendships' than 'business contacts'.

So where do you begin to build your network? You need to think of your network along two dimensions: depth and breadth. A deep network is one where the relationships within the network are strong and mutually recognized as such. A broad network encompasses a large number of relationships.

Building deep networks

To build a strong, deep network, start with your attitude and behaviours. More than anything else, your attitude and behaviours determine your ability to forge strong relationships. To build strong networks, networks based on real relationships, heed the following.

Be real

One of the executives whom I interviewed from General Electric forwarded an article that Jack Welch, the former CEO of General Electric, wrote for the *Wall Street Journal* (28 October 2004, page A14) in the run-up to the 2004 presidential election. In this article, Jack recommended that the electorate ask five questions about the presidential candidates when deciding for whom to vote. The first of these five questions was: 'Is he real?' Here is a quote from that article:

> *When I was at GE, we would occasionally encounter a very successful executive who just could not be promoted to the next level. In the early days, we would struggle with our reasoning. The person demonstrated the right values and made the numbers, but usually his people did not connect with him. What was wrong? Finally, we figured out that these people always had a certain phoniness about them. They pretended to be something they were not – more in control, more upbeat, more savvy than they really were. They didn't sweat. They didn't cry. They squirmed in their own skin, playing a role of their own inventing.*

Granted, Jack is talking about middle-level managers here but, if there is one resounding message that comes through from all the executives interviewed about their first-rung career, it is this need to be 'real'.

Christy Roberts of Intuit believes that she was effective at building her network because she did not try to be anyone other than herself. She maintained her fun sense of humour and let herself enjoy being around people. Unsurprisingly, people liked to be around Christy, and her network grew from there.

> She was effective at building her network because she did not try to be anyone other than herself.

Renee Jordan of Ford calls it being 'genuine'. She argues that networks are ineffective if people feel you are only becoming acquainted for personal gain. This is why the common concept of networking is not that important. In a room full of strangers, if you are visibly speaking to lots of people and doing little more than making contact before moving on, people will struggle to find you genuine. There is something about making too much effort and forcing the interaction.

A classmate of mine from Harvard Business School reinforces this viewpoint. Even at Harvard Business School he remembers experiencing a few of these 'room prowler' types at so-called 'networking events'. He calls them 'social butterflies', who pass from one person to another, chirping about how great it is to meet you or see you and then disappearing. Certainly, they would meet everyone in the room, but my classmate soon returned to the people with whom he was connecting on a 'real' level. While he interacted with fewer people, he walked away not with 20 weak contacts but with the seeds of two or three real relationships.

In Chapter 1, we discussed the need to possess and exhibit certain attitudinal qualities to succeed, but this does not mean that you need to be someone other than yourself. These attitudinal qualities are indeed central to being successful, but they can be developed and exist in many different personalities. You should not fall into the trap of thinking that, by being yourself or 'real', you can indulge your weaknesses.

Focus on individual relationships

When it comes down to it, effective networks are no more than a set of individual relationships. Consequently, a network is only strong if the relationships are

> When it comes down to it, effective networks are no more than a set of individual relationships.

strong. Strong networks, where you can call on someone for a quick favour such as providing access to someone you cannot reach on your own or to answer a question on some work issue, work better if they are based on real relationships.

Luis Costa of Procter & Gamble is one of many executives who view their networks as a collection of real relationships. In his job of supporting the brand management of a major washing powder, Luis had to work with several departments, whether it was to discuss new promotional material with the sales department or to resolve business plan and budget issues with the finance department. By having real relationships with these people, he was able to call on them when he needed and feel confident that they would deliver on his behalf.

Lawrence Fowler of GlaxoSmithKline is another example of someone who emphasizes the importance of relationships. He argues that people need to feel that you respect them and want to get to know them on a personal level, not only to make their acquaintance in case they may prove useful to you.

Renee Jordan of Ford goes one step further and argues that you need to include a social element to build effective networks. She explains that someone who is more sociable, who shows a genuine interest in the other person and talks about other things than purely professional matters when appropriate, is far more likely to forge a real relationship.

Recall that Mike Sandler of McMaster-Carr learned the names and the personal backgrounds of over 35 people in an administrative department. He was able to start off every interaction by asking after the other person. He was not a fake; he did not show interest only to increase cooperation. But of course, because he showed a genuine interest in them, these people were more cooperative and helpful as a consequence.

Deliver professionally

Ultimately, it does not matter how adroit you are interpersonally. If you do not deliver professionally, your ability to build professional relationships will suffer. As Elizabeth Baker of Arthur Andersen puts it: 'People have to have confidence in you, and trust in your ability to execute.'

Ultimately, it does not matter how adroit you are interpersonally. If you do not deliver professionally, your ability to build professional relationships will suffer.

Mark Jackson of Dell built his networks with the explicit aim of improving his performance. Working in a manufacturing environment where he was charged with managing blue-collar workers and improving operations, Mark realized that he needed to understand the priorities of several executives from different departments, such as scheduling, delivery and operations. He set up meetings with each of these executives to understand precisely what their main priorities were, the pressures they were under and what ultimately motivated them with respect to their decision making.

He implicitly developed relationships with them and learned how they operated and, when it came to proposing changes to the metrics to create greater alignment across the departments, Mark was able to leverage the relationships to both refine the proposal and gain buy-in for it. The proposal was ultimately accepted, operational performance improved substantially, Mark looked like a star and everyone else looked good too. Was this classic 'networking'? No. But does Mark have a powerful network? Yes.

Be helpful

In your job, most of your interaction with people is ultimately work-related. While adding a social component to the interaction by asking after the other person and remembering details of his or her personal life certainly helps the relationship grow, you need to follow up professionally and be helpful to ensure a true foundation to the relationship. People remember you if you help them and they feel they can rely on you. Go the extra mile too, and think how you can be helpful beyond their request.

Steven Bond of Ralph Lauren makes himself the 'go-to' person by being as helpful as possible. When someone from another department asks him for something, he makes sure he delivers and he makes sure he delivers quickly. He often goes the extra mile, providing extra information or more contacts than requested. Naturally, because his colleagues knew that Steven was helpful they always returned to him whenever they wanted any other favour. These executives sang Steven's praises and contributed to his word-of-mouth reputation, and were more than willing to cooperate and return favours whenever he needed something from them or their department.

In the context of a network, you need to rely much more heavily on a quid pro quo process of cooperation. A larger network can help you delegate, but you need to have built that cooperation by being helpful in the first place. By being helpful and responding to the needs of others within your network, you will engender their good

> A larger network can help you delegate, but you need to have built that cooperation by being helpful in the first place.

favour and create in them a willingness to cooperate and help in return. It is important that you are not too clinical in this process of quid pro quo. You best develop such reciprocity not by keeping a log of favours done and returned but by trying to be helpful yourself.

Lawrence Fowler of GlaxoSmithKline recognized the implicit quid pro quo involved in these professional interactions, and he too emphasizes the importance of not keeping score or being too clinical in choosing when and to whom to be helpful. Obviously, you should not let anyone take undue advantage of you, but helping people is a great way to get them 'on-side' and build a relationship.

Ask for advice

One of the quickest ways to build a relationship is to ask for advice or coaching. As always, it is important to be sincere and to appeal genuinely to a particular person because you believe he or she is able to help you. Do not appear simply to be trying to curry favour.

Renee Jordan of Ford found that, by asking people for their opinion or advice on a matter, she was able to demonstrate respect for people. People like to feel that their opinions count and are naturally more inclined to get on with someone who values their opinion.

Jack Reardon of American Medical Security frequently asked for advice because he recognized that his colleagues had significant experience and knowledge that he had not yet gained. He benefited from their advice in terms of learning, impressed his colleagues and superiors with his appetite and enthusiasm for learning and developed a network with strong relationships.

Maintain meaningful contact

The reason why the 'contact only' type of network is so weak is that most people do very little after making initial contact. They only follow up if there is some specific thing that they want or need from

The reason why the 'contact only' type of network is so weak is that most people do very little after making initial contact.

their contact, which further accentuates the sense of 'being used'.

Even with a relationship approach to networking, you need to make an effort to maintain contact. Many network relationships grow out of working relationships that are often relatively short-lived – a particular project or job assignment. A new project or new assignment means that you no longer have the same direct interaction and so you have to maintain contact proactively if you want to prevent the relationship from becoming dormant.

Mary Peters of Microsoft emphasizes the need to maintain the relationships within a network. She explains that, since networks are about relationships, you have to make the effort. She points out that maintaining relationships is not particularly onerous; an e-mail, a phone call, a cup of coffee or a lunch every few weeks works fine.

Elizabeth Baker of Arthur Andersen agrees. She believes that relationships develop when you make that bit of effort to stay in contact, particularly when you no longer have a formal or direct working interaction.

Building broad networks

When it comes to creating broad networks, you have to meet new people. You do not have to be a 'room prowler' vacuuming up everyone's contact details, but you should try to get to know a small number of people well in any given setting. Over time, your network will grow significantly if you take advantage of these opportunities.

> You do not have to be a 'room prowler' vacuuming up everyone's contact details, but you should try to get to know a small number of people well in any given setting.

Build 360-degree networks

Too many executives focus on networking with people who are more senior than they are. The cleverer executives recognize that their peer group is also of vital importance. Your future boss may be one of your peers, or a peer may prove instrumental to an important project for which you are held accountable. The cleverest executives, however, seek to build broad networks with people above and below them – they develop a '360-degree' network. For a first-rung executive, this includes support staff, who are effectively professional subordinates, whether they are the people working in the post room, the people cleaning the office space, blue-collar staff on the factory floor or administrative support staff.

Dan Barker of US Robotics is a big advocate of building a broad 360-degree network. He argues that you never can tell when people may be able to contribute, and your ability to facilitate their contribution is vastly improved by having a relationship with them.

Andy Sage of Panasonic is another who emphasizes the 360-degree network. He recognizes that, within a company, everybody has a role to play, which is why people were hired in the first place. By forging relationships with as many people as possible, he is better able to marshal resources and leverage relationships.

Take advantage of social opportunities

You do not have to be a social butterfly to network. You do not have to be able to walk into a room and be the centre of attention and speak to everyone in that room to

> You have to put yourself in situations where you meet new people to grow your network.

network. But you have to put yourself in situations where you meet new people to grow your network.

Ryan Yapp of Constellation Energy suggests taking advantage of any social situation with your work colleagues. He says he has created many good relationships 'over a couple of beers, or going for a dinner'. He argues that the casual nature of the interaction supports effective relationship building.

Mary Peters of Microsoft believes that eating at your desk may be good for 'face-time' purposes, but if you head to the company café and sit down at a table of people you have not met before you have a great opportunity to make new friends. She adds that, given the limited number of people typically sitting around a lunch table, you can get to develop meaningful relationships.

Set up meetings

Another way to initiate opportunities to build relationships is to set up meetings directly with people. Sometimes you can set up appointments with the sole purpose of introducing yourself, but you are better off seeking to use such meetings to learn more about the business and how the people you meet fit into the business.

Adrian White of United Health Insurance is an advocate of setting up lots of one-to-one meetings with people and peppering them with questions. As he says, 'Just getting people in a room and asking them lots of questions is a great way to learn about the business, to get your face known and to start developing relationships.'

Mark Jackson of Dell agrees with the principle of setting up meetings. He schedules 30 minutes with a broad set of people, including people from his own team, his boss's peers and executives from different departments too. He uses these meetings to understand what motivates different people, what performance objectives they have to meet and what they prioritize. He believes that, if he can get inside their heads and understand them as individuals, he is better able to focus on the things that matter most to them. The process of getting to understand them, of course, helps Mark build network relationships, relationships that he is then able to strengthen by serving people's needs better.

A word of caution here – this approach works in some organizations only, typically in organizations that have a very open atmosphere and where people are generally not operating under high stress levels. Some executives in more fast-paced organizations such as investment banks warn against wasting busy people's time. One simple way to test whether people in your organization are amenable to this approach is to see if your organization has a long-hours culture. If it does, usually that means people are working under pressure, hence the long hours, and their willingness to take part in non-essential meetings will be limited.

Be flexible with assignments

Many companies rotate their employees through different divisions and across different locations. Even if not part of an official rotation programme, relocation is an increasingly common occurrence for today's corporate executive. Many of the executives surveyed have had to work extensively in different cities and different countries.

David Bruce of Aramark believes his flexibility to take on diverse geographic assignments contributed greatly to his ability to expand his network within the company. From the outset, he demonstrated a willingness to move to any part of the company. While relocating is often less than ideal in the larger context of your life, it is a great way to build your network and demonstrate your commitment at the same time.

Some companies with a number of different offices, particularly if they are international, almost have an unwritten rule that to progress you have to earn 'international spurs'.

While relocating is often less than ideal in the larger context of your life, it is a great way to build your network and demonstrate your commitment at the same time.

John Abrahams of Credit Suisse First Boston has clocked up significant experience in both New York and Los Angeles in the United States, São Paolo in Brazil, and London. He has built a strong international network and, given the international nature of many of the prime deals, he is a great fit to work on them and further accelerate his performance. He continues to rise up the ranks.

In a nutshell – How to build your network

■ Be real.

■ Focus on individual relationships.

■ Deliver professionally.

■ Be helpful.

■ Ask for advice.

■ Maintain meaningful contact.

■ Build 360-degree networks.

■ Take advantage of social opportunities.

■ Set up meetings (but be respectful of people's time).

■ Be flexible with assignments.

8

Find your mentors

John Spender joined a major US investment bank from Harvard Business School as one of the worst financial market recessions in history began. At this investment bank, John joined a class of more than 100 other MBA graduates entering the investment banking division. Over the next two years, John was one of the few people in his class who was not laid off as part of continued retrenchment in the financial sector. Now you might think that, because John was a Harvard Business School graduate, his job was always going to be pretty secure. But you would be wrong. Plenty of MBA graduates from Harvard and other top business schools did not survive the financial market purge of 2001 and 2002. All in all, John survived seven rounds of lay-offs. Count them – seven! Not only did he survive the lay-offs, but he was the top-ranking executive in his class. John is a very talented executive, but if you ask him for the key factors in his success he will say that one of the most important was finding a good mentor.

As with a social network, where one has many friends but only a small number of special friends, a professional network should include some special relationships. These special relationships should include relationships with mentors, because mentors play a very important role in your immediate and long-term career. Many of those surveyed for this book, across all kinds of industries, not only within financial services, felt strongly that having one or more good mentors made a big difference in their early careers. They also believe that mentoring relationships do not just happen. You have to work at them. You cannot force a mentoring relationship if certain ingredients are not present, but neither should you expect mentoring relationships to happen on their own. You might be one of the lucky ones to be 'adopted' by a mentor, but you would be foolish to leave things solely to chance.

In this chapter we will cover the following topics:

> You cannot force a mentoring relationship if certain ingredients are not present, but neither should you expect mentoring relationships to happen on their own.

■ why mentors are important;
■ identifying potential mentors;
■ cultivating and getting the most out of mentoring relationships;
■ the junior mentor.

Why mentors are important

Mentoring relationships are the modern equivalent to the apprentice–master relationship. They are the vehicles through which senior executives pass on the benefit of their experience to first-rungers. However, the big difference between mentoring

> Mentoring relationships are the modern equivalent to the apprentice–master relationship. They are the vehicles through which senior executives pass on the benefit of their experience to first-rungers.

and apprenticeship is that there is no formal process for setting up mentoring relationships. While some companies institute formal mentoring mechanisms, ultimately the task lies with you – you need to identify potential mentors within your company and you have to develop relationships with them yourself. While it may lack any contractual obligation, a good mentoring relationship can still bring many of the benefits of the old apprentice–master relationship and more.

James Edwards of Novartis describes mentors as 'phenomenally important'. In fact, most executives believe that mentors are critical and highlight several if not all of the following benefits.

On-the-job and long-term career advice

Mentors are among the most important resources for learning when you are on the first rung. Renee Jordan had four mentors during the course of her first few years at Ford, all of whom were instrumental in progressing her professional development. Renee benefited from her mentors' counsel on how to manage the challenging dynamic of being a female executive in a male-dominated blue-collar environment. When she had specific questions on operational issues on the plant floor, her mentors were always available for advice. On one occasion, Renee wanted to make a controversial hiring decision and was worried that she lacked the support of her colleagues. Renee used one of her mentors as a sounding board and ultimately he instilled Renee with the confidence that her decision was final and would be respected. Renee's mentors also offered her advice on which opportunities within Ford were most suited for her in growing as an executive in the broader context of her career. One such piece of advice led to Renee accepting an exciting overseas placement in Europe, where she gained excellent international exposure and learned a new language. Renee became a top performer at Ford and has continued to have significant career success.

Career and job opportunities

Not only can they advise on which opportunities to pursue, but mentors can help to provide opportunities by recommending you, supporting your placement on new assignments or directly providing opportunities themselves.

> Mentors can help to provide opportunities by recommending you, supporting your placement on new assignments or directly providing opportunities themselves.

Often, the best career opportunities offer exposure to different parts of the company and different people and allow you to broaden and develop your skill set. Usually, your mentors know your skill set very well and therefore understand which opportunities are most suitable. The best mentors, though, will recognize the opportunities where you can grow, not only where they see a match for your skill set.

Matthew Carmichael, also of Ford, had mentors who actively supported his overseas placement and gave him valuable exposure to Ford's international business that allowed him to develop a strong understanding of foreign markets. Luke Patella of Bain & Company developed his client presentation skills through participation in important client meetings and attributes the invitations to these meetings and the opportunity to present to an individual mentor. Roger Black of USAID thanks his mentors for supporting him in his career even after he had left the organization. They provided him with leads and contacts and supported him as he explored his next career move after graduating from business school.

Mentors can even provide opportunities at new companies. When mentors join new companies they frequently seek to take their most valued team members with them. A mentor of Dan Barker at Ameritech did exactly this – after joining a new company he courted Dan for a new position.

Support during reviews and evaluations

Many firms claim that they have a meritocratic review and evaluation process. Not one single executive interviewed believed that his or her company was truly meritocratic. The executives also

> Having one or more senior people pulling for them during reviews and evaluations was critical to ensuring their recognition as high performers.

agreed that having one or more senior people pulling for them during reviews and evaluations was critical to ensuring their recognition as high performers. One executive even discovered that her firm had a round table of senior executives to discuss staff rankings even before the formal process of 360-degree feedback (comprehensive feedback from seniors, subordinates and peers) had begun. Jeff Callahan of Schroders attributes a significant portion of his recognition at review time to his mentors. As another executive put it, 'Having someone banging the table for me at review time made a difference. It got me ranked and prevented me from being among those fired.'

Just as mentors influence reviews and evaluations, they also influence when you get promoted and into which positions. It was no coincidence that Steven Bond of Ralph Lauren was promoted at the same time as his mentor on more than one occasion.

Future references

Almost all of those executives interviewed who went to business school relied on their mentors to provide their references. One of my mentors from my days in investment banking wrote my references for business school applications and, to this day, I still count him as a current mentor and a future source for references.

Projection of a positive reputation

As we discussed in Chapter 7, one of the most powerful forms of marketing is through word of mouth. Your reputation – your personal brand – is critical to your success. We spend more time on managing your personal brand in Chapter 9. However, for now, understand that mentors, like your networks, play an important role in projecting your reputation through word of mouth. Carl Moran works for General Electric (GE), one of the largest firms in the world. GE is not just large, but it is a conglomerate, which makes it even more decentralized than most large firms, because it has so many different, autonomous businesses. Carl's mentors played a critical role in projecting his reputation to corporate head office and getting him known across the decentralized firm.

Psychological support

You may think that all of the successful executives who contributed to this book were so capable and confident that they never had to struggle. You would be wrong. All of the executives faced difficult times in their careers. It was not only in their early days, when they were on a very steep learning curve. In many instances, they found themselves in unfamiliar territory and suffering lapses of confidence or moments of despair. Their mentors were there to help them through these difficult periods.

This is a pretty compelling list of benefits and it is only partly tied to your performance. You may also notice that two of the benefits (career and job opportunities, and projection of a positive reputation) are the same as those discussed in Chapter 7 – this should serve to remind you that your chances of finding good mentors increase with the breadth and depth of your network.

However, mentors can be much more of a direct influence in your career than a network because, by definition, they take a direct interest in you. When it comes to creating job and career opportunities, for example, a good mentor will fight on your behalf to get you on to a particular project or into a new job, while standard network contacts are more likely to 'suggest' you or at best 'support' you.

Nevertheless, the list of benefits that a mentor brings suggests the question: what does the mentor get in return for providing all of these considerable benefits? This may come as a surprise to you, but some mentors feel an emotional reward from helping, supporting and developing first-rungers. Call it the 'feel-good factor' if you will, but it is genuine and it exists even in the cut-throat world of business. These mentors look for nothing in return; they are nurturing by instinct. Some executives had several mentors who were natural 'nurturers' and seemed almost to adopt them.

A different kind of mentor, but often as effective, is one with whom you have a genuine working relationship. This mentor gains your loyalty and commitment and relies on the work and service you provide. Steven Bond of Ralph Lauren had one such mentor and called their relationship 'symbiotic'. His mentor relied on him and trusted him to get important work done and to make him look good. This is where performance is important in developing mentors but, as we discuss later, it is not the only factor.

While most mentoring relationships are symbiotic early on, and many effective ones remain symbiotic, the ultimate mentoring relationships evolve beyond symbiosis. For Dan Barker of Ameritech, his mentoring relationships reached a point where his mentors offered advice, support and opportunities without receiving any discernible reciprocal benefit.

How to identify potential mentors

Many companies recognize the importance of mentoring and have instituted formal mentoring programmes. Often, they allocate a first-runger to a senior member of staff or adopt buddy systems between more and less experienced first-rungers. At best, these work modestly well, because effective mentoring relationships do not develop only by pairing two people together. An effective mentoring relationship requires certain ingredients.

Unfortunately, identifying a mentor is not like shopping for a car. You cannot walk into a showroom of mentors and pick the shiniest model with all the latest features. You need a combination of luck and proactivity to uncover potential mentors. But even before being proactive

about developing a mentor, you
need to know whether a potential
mentor has the right ingredients
for an effective mentoring relationship. The following are the
most important questions to ask
to identify these ingredients.

> Before being proactive about
> developing a mentor, you need to
> know whether a potential mentor
> has the right ingredients for an
> effective mentoring relationship.

Does the potential mentor have influence?

Mentors are only in a position to offer certain of the benefits described
in the previous section if they are in a position of influence. Mentors
cannot support you during review and evaluation periods if their
opinion carries no weight. They need influence to get you promotions
and pay increases.

One executive was fortunate enough to start out his career in the
European corporate headquarters and forged lasting relationships with
some of the most senior executives in the company. Some of them
continue to support him to this day. However, as we discussed in
Chapter 6, you should not confuse formal authority with influence.
While formal authority usually comes with direct influence, influence
does not always require formal authority. When I was a junior banker,
I spotted an executive who was still a mid-level banker, but I saw that
this executive had the ears of those who did have significant influence
and could therefore exert indirect influence on my behalf. He did and,
of my class, I had one of the best experiences in terms of the number of
live deals I worked on and financially.

Is the potential mentor hungry?

Do not make the mistake of going after only the most senior, influential
figures for mentors. It is great if you can become the CEO's, or the
new star senior executive's, favourite first-runger, but in many instances
he or she will have little time for you. Most mentoring relationships
are symbiotic – your mentor gets something out of the relationship
too. Those mid- to senior-level executives who are still very hungry for
further success in their own careers often make great mentors, as they
need support from below to help them progress. They are frequently
loyal and, when they get promoted, they usually take their best staff
with them.

John Abrahams of Credit Suisse First Boston recognized one such potential mentor and made sure that he worked with him on a number of deals. This particular mentor was the least senior managing director in the

> Those mid- to senior-level executives who are still very hungry for further success in their own careers often make great mentors, as they need support from below to help them progress.

group, but within a couple of years became head of the group. John saw that this managing director was hungry and because he commanded professional respect not only from John, but also from a number of other people, John believed that he was 'backing a good horse'.

Kirk Williams of Chrysler believes hunger can be even more important than influence. He argues that, if mentors are talented and hungry, influence will come as they progress. The big difference is that talented and hungry potential mentors need people to help them succeed and therefore are more likely to reward those who help them than someone already very senior who does not have much to gain. As one executive interviewed put it, in reference to why his mentor was so successful and why he became influential, 'A hungry dog hunts best.'

Do you have chemistry?

A mentoring relationship is like any other meaningful relationship: it hinges on chemistry. You need to relate to your mentor on a personal level. You need to like your mentor. Similarly, your mentor needs to relate to you. When Jack Reardon started out at American Medical Security, he hit it off with the divisional CEO even during his initial interview. Jack recalls that he knew they were going to get on well at one specific point during the interview. The interview was at nine in the evening and, to get to it, Jack had driven up to the company headquarters through a major snowstorm. During the interview, the divisional CEO, appreciative of Jack's effort to make the interview, offered Jack use of the company's dining facilities. Jack politely declined and said that he had brought a packed dinner. Jack remembers that the divisional CEO was initially taken aback by the fact that Jack had frugally prepared his own packed dinner. The divisional CEO even commented that few executives brought their own packed meals any more. It turned out that the CEO was similarly frugal and, from that point on, the divisional CEO and Jack were kindred spirits, which formed the foundation of an enduring mentoring relationship.

Do not try to force chemistry; ultimately, even if potential mentors have the other ideal mentoring attributes, if they do not click with you or do not want to mentor you there is not much you can do. However, while chemistry may be

Do not try to force chemistry; ultimately, even if potential mentors have the other ideal mentoring attributes, if they do not click with you or do not want to mentor you there is not much you can do.

something that you cannot force, your ability to get on with people affects the chances of finding and building chemistry. I am sure you have friends who possess the ability to relate to all kinds of people. They seem to develop chemistry with everyone. If you take a closer look at why they are so likeable, you will usually find the answer in their interpersonal skills and attitude and behaviours. Roger Black of USAID is one such individual. He seems to have a knack for getting on with all kinds of people. His mentoring relationships were not even working relationships; they were primarily built around personal chemistry. If you ask Roger his secret, he does indeed point to his interpersonal skills and attitude but also mentions flexibility – the ability to adapt to different personalities. In fact, he is an advocate of Dale Carnegie's *How to Win Friends and Influence People*, and believes that the kind of interpersonal skills and attitudes espoused in this book are critical to building chemistry with most people.

Do you have exposure?

All relationships require some kind of exposure between individuals at their outset. Most frequently, you will gain this exposure through real working relationships. Jack Reardon and the divisional CEO may have had chemistry, but the divisional CEO only became Jack's mentor because the two of them worked together on a regular basis. This working relationship was important for Jack, both to cement a personal relationship and to demonstrate his potential. Without some kind of exposure, your mentor will struggle to appreciate not only your potential as an executive, but also your potential to contribute to him or her. Mentors need to perform and feel fulfilled in their jobs, just like first-rungers. Do not underestimate how important you are to a mentor's performance, progress and sense of fulfilment.

Most often the mentor in a working relationship is a boss. In fact, most executives interviewed had at least one mentor who was a direct boss. However, there are usually several layers of management above a first-runger (if only the career ladder had two rungs) and you should not limit yourself to direct bosses. Renee Jordan at Ford worked in a relatively small team under her direct boss. Consequently, she also had a meaningful working relationship with her boss's boss, and it was with this person that she developed her main mentoring relationship, although she still classified her direct boss as a mentor too. Look at the direct reporting lines. Often you will find that you have working relationships with executives much further up the reporting structure than your direct boss. So long as you have meaningful exposure to these executives, view them as potential mentor candidates too.

Even though it is most likely that you will develop mentoring relationships within your division, do not limit your search for potential mentors here. In many companies, you have to work across a number of divisional boundaries. Steven Bond at Ralph Lauren had to work with executives from the design, supply and real estate departments. Despite no direct reporting line to any of these executives, Steven recognized enough foundation to develop a mentoring relationship with a senior figure in the supply department.

Roger Black of USAID argues that exposure to mentors need not come from working relationships at all, particularly if the mentors are very senior. He explains that very senior mentors nurture of their own free will, since there is little scope for them to receive reciprocal benefit from a first-runger. They see mentoring relationships more in personal terms than professional terms. He believes that asking to work with these very senior mentors can actually undermine the personal relationships. Another executive describes his exposure to senior executives as a further consequence of physical proximity. Not only was he located on the same floor as a number of very senior executives, but he sat right next to the lifts: whenever anyone walked into or out of the lifts they had to walk by his desk. His mentoring relationships grew from the daily interaction with senior executives that ensued.

Do you have professional respect?

John Abrahams of Credit Suisse First Boston says he must have professional respect for a person before he can consider him or her as a potential mentor. He lists job performance, integrity and judgement as prerequisites that command professional respect. Without these prerequisites, John does not trust the mentor to provide good and honest advice. Jack Reardon of American Medical Security agrees. He views mentors as role models, and he only aspires to emulate those whom he professionally respects.

How to cultivate and get the most out of mentoring relationships

Some effective mentoring relationships develop of their own accord – the relationship begins by chance and happens to possess the necessary ingredients, and the first-runger does everything right. However, many of the executives interviewed explicitly recognized potential mentors and went after them proactively. They followed specific principles to cultivate effective mentoring relationships. When you enter your first job, actively look for potential mentors and, when you find one, consider the following approaches to create effective mentoring relationships.

Build your network

As we have already discussed, the first step to finding a mentor is to build your network. Mentor relationships are special relationships within your network, but they grow from a normal network relationship. The larger your network, the more chance of both discovering and encountering a potential mentor.

Ask for work

If your best chance of gaining exposure to potential mentors is to work with them, then you should ask to work with them. When Carl Moran first joined GE, he was put under the charge of a poor manager. He was unhappy with his experience and felt he was not learning. He went back to corporate headquarters and insisted that he be teamed up with 'one of the best three managers in the company'. Obviously, this was a very bold move; you should be very careful about going over your current boss's head. Nevertheless, Carl took his fortune into his own hands and was successfully assigned to an excellent manager with whom he forged a lasting mentoring relationship.

Ask to work for someone and you take control of your working life. Wait for the right time, use the appropriate channels and be sensitive to your existing boss and colleagues if you are making a visible move. Whenever you ask to work for someone new, follow one critical rule: explain your rationale only in terms of what you wish to gain, not what you wish to avoid. For example, suppose you are working with a bad manager and are looking for a better manager. Never say that you want to get away from the bad manager because he or she is useless. Instead, show gratitude and appreciation for your experience so far, position your request in terms of your need for a different experience, and focus on how this new experience ultimately benefits your company. I make no bones about it: this is 'spin'; but, as we discuss in the final chapter, managing perception is vital. Your challenge is to get the best experience and work with the best people without alienating anyone, even those you may not like or respect.

Sometimes, it is not feasible to ask to work with a potential mentor. You might be on a fixed rotation programme where your assignments are non-negotiable. If your potential mentor lies outside your working environment, still do not give up on trying to develop relationships. One of the key elements of the working relationship that leads to mentoring is exposure, and there are other ways you can seek to gain exposure.

Most companies have many ancillary activities such as recruiting, conferences and organizing company events and office parties. These provide excellent forums for gaining exposure to potential mentors. When I was a junior banker, I participated in organizing the office Christmas party and benefited from strengthening my relationships with potential mentors.

Over-deliver

Once you have managed to create the opportunity to work with a potential mentor, you must over-deliver. You must make yourself invaluable to your potential mentor. You must distinguish yourself from your peers through superior

> You must over-deliver. You must make yourself invaluable to your potential mentor. You must distinguish yourself from your peers through superior performance.

performance. Renee Jordan of Ford worked hard from day one to build trust and instil her potential mentor with confidence. Jack Reardon of American Medical Security says that the first impression counts the most, and found that the most critical time to over-deliver is early on in the working relationship. Chris Moritz of Teligent agrees; he sees a direct correlation between hard work and performance and believes that the time to perform is early on in the mentoring relationship to establish credibility and trust. We covered commitment and enthusiasm in Chapter 1, but, if there is a time to turn it on, it is starting off with a new mentor. Work longer hours, double- and triple-check your work, do more than is asked of you, beat deadlines and look for every opportunity to make your potential mentor's job and life easier. Over-deliver early to ensure a great first impression and to lock in a strong relationship.

Be loyal

As a first-runger, almost everyone is your boss. You may have a clear single direct reporting line to someone other than your mentor, and you have to fulfil your duties

> Make your mentor your number one priority whenever you can and show him or her unwavering loyalty.

within the scope of that reporting line, but make your mentor your number one priority whenever you can and show him or her unwavering loyalty. Whenever Harriet Giggs of PricewaterhouseCoopers has any spare capacity, she offers it to her mentor first. If she has ideas for business opportunities, she discusses them with her mentor before anybody else. If she has important information to share, she makes sure that her mentor hears it first. Harriet shows her mentor loyalty because she understands that loyalty creates loyalty and, by looking out for her mentor, her mentor looks out for her. Be loyal to your mentors and make them recognize your loyalty.

Seek advice and feedback

One of the key benefits mentors provide is on-the-job coaching and long-term career advice. If you are lucky, they will automatically nurture you. However, do not wait for your mentor to volunteer advice and feedback. Take the first step and proactively seek advice and feedback from your mentor. The very act of seeking advice and feedback shapes your interaction towards one of a mentoring relationship. By seeking advice and feedback, you demonstrate commitment and enthusiasm for your job and respect for your mentor, making him or her inclined to coach you.

Melissa Castle of Honeywell believes the best way to ask for feedback and advice, particularly as the mentoring relationship is developing, is to avoid speaking in generalities such as 'How am I doing?' If you ask non-specific questions like this, you run the risk of being seen to fish for compliments. Furthermore, if you speak in generalities, your mentor is more likely to answer in similar generalities. I have seen colleagues ask 'How am I doing?' and often the only response they receive is 'Fine' – not a particularly illuminating piece of feedback or one that instils them with any confidence. Focus on advice and feedback on specific issues. Melissa found that asking specific questions, such as whether she had gone about making a decision to resolve an issue on the production floor in the right way, was far more likely to lead to answers that helped her in her career.

Keep regular contact

While most mentoring relationships are borne from direct working relationships, great mentoring relationships outlast working relationships. Most executives still regard many of their early mentors as mentors today. Dan Barker of Ameritech still seeks advice and coaching from early mentors, even though they no longer work in the same company. One executive works in a very exciting role for one of his former mentors who is now the CEO of another company. These mentoring relationships are the ultimate success story, as they have grown beyond a purely symbiotic relationship.

The junior mentor

Many of the executives surveyed and interviewed for this book highlighted good mentors as a critical factor in their first-rung success. However, most of these executives talked about mentors who were significantly more senior than they were, whether direct bosses or bosses' bosses or other senior executives. This chapter has focused on these senior mentors. In this final section, however, we discuss a second type of mentor – the junior mentor – whom a few executives mentioned as being extremely important to them. I am one of those executives whose early career substantially benefited from having a junior mentor, and my research for this book leads me to believe that even successful first-rungers underutilize junior mentors.

When I first started out in investment banking, I was as green as they came. I had no work experience of any kind. While my university friends had worked for well-known companies, I had played in tennis tournaments during the summer holidays. My degree was in chemistry and molecular biology and was not a huge amount of help in finance. I was fortunate enough to join a firm that had a four-month training programme but, even after this programme, I still had much to learn. I joined a small team consisting of a director and a second-year analyst. That second-year analyst proved to be my first mentor – my junior mentor. He may not have been able to provide the full list of benefits a senior mentor can offer. However, he not only rescued me from going wrong on many occasions, but he taught me how to master the fundamentals of my job.

I remember, late one evening, I was trying to do something called 'comparable company analysis'. The basic premise of comparable company analysis is that you can figure out how much a private company is worth by comparing it to publicly listed companies that have observable market values. The process involves going through the accounts of public companies and the private company you are trying to value and plugging their financial information into a spreadsheet. There were many subtleties to doing this properly, including knowing where in the accounts and financial statements to find specific pieces of information and knowing what adjustments to make to each company's accounts to make the accounting treatment of each company consistent. The output of the analysis was a set of financial ratios that could be used to imply a valuation for the private company.

On this particular occasion, when I showed the output of all the financial ratios to the second-year analyst, there were many numbers that I could not explain. I had a meeting at 9 am the following morning, I was tired and flustered and I was going to look like a fool if I could not provide robust explanations. The second-year analyst spent the next hour going through my entire spreadsheet, uncovering mistakes that I had made, helping me understand why certain numbers looked odd and preparing me so that I could shine in the morning meeting. By the end of that year, I had become so proficient that I became well known for my comparable company analysis skills and was even asked to teach the next incoming class on the subject. It was all because of that second-year analyst.

When Carl Moran of GE was new to his job, he too was unfamiliar with many of the basic tasks of the job. He recalls his boss asking him to draw up a pivot table of some data using Microsoft Excel. Carl had no idea how to perform this analysis and relied on a junior mentor to teach him. His skills developed much faster than they would have had he had to muddle through on his own, and his rapid mastery allowed him to conduct better analysis and earn the recognition of his bosses.

The reason junior mentors are lifesavers is because they have just gone through the very experience you are now going through. They understand the difficulties and the worries, and they have learned

> The reason junior mentors are lifesavers is because they have just gone through the very experience you are now going through.

how to handle the first-rung job. I remember, when I was a second-year analyst, that my classmates and I were more effective than brand-new associates out of the top business schools. They may have earned more money than us, and they were more experienced, but we had the inside track and we knew exactly how everything worked. In fact, as we discussed in Chapter 6, sometimes a strange dynamic existed where a second-year analyst mentored an older, more senior and better-paid first-year associate for his or her first few weeks.

The second big reason why junior mentors are so valuable is that they provide a relatively risk-free environment in which to learn. A junior mentor can answer all of your stupid questions and spot your mistakes without any real consequence other than helping you learn. This may not always be the case with more senior mentors.

When you start out on the first rung, look out for more experienced first-rungers and seek their help when you need to figure out how to do a specific task or when you do not know where to look or whom to approach to get hold of information. A junior mentor is far more proficient at explaining these day-to-day tasks than a senior mentor, because the junior mentor has to perform the same type of job as you do.

In a nutshell – How to find your mentors

■ Mentors are important because they provide support and advice on a range of issues.

■ Identify potential mentors carefully – do they have influence, are they hungry and do you have chemistry?

■ Cultivate and get the most out of mentoring relationships by asking for work, over-delivering, being loyal, seeking advice and feedback, and keeping regular contact.

■ Do not forget about the junior mentor.

9

Become politically savvy

Most executives interviewed believe that, regardless of how good your attitude is or how well you demonstrate mastery of the fundamentals, and even if you are supported by a strong network and influential mentors, other factors can still significantly influence your career trajectory.

Most of these 'other' factors highlighted by executives fall into the realm of 'politics and perception'. Politics, in the context of organizations, is ultimately about the complex interactions between a large number of individuals, all with their own means and degrees of influence, and all with their own personal agendas and motivations. These interactions forge a shifting web of relationships, alliances and oppositions that ultimately create a politically influenced environment. Perception, in the context of politics, is about how individuals view each other, most importantly from the perspective of their own personal agendas. For example, whether people perceive someone as important, unimportant or detrimental to their personal agendas may have significant bearing on relevant decisions.

This chapter focuses on teaching you to become politically savvy. In particular, it focuses on the following topics:

- organizational culture and two organizational myths;
- handling politics for first-rungers;
- controlling perception by building a personal brand.

Organizational culture and two organizational myths

Most organizations like to regard themselves as having a 'culture'. A culture is a way of doing things, a protocol for behaviour, or a modus operandi for how to conduct business. Some organizations have very strong cultures, where deviation from organizational norms is rare. Others have weaker cultures where there is a high dispersion of individual behaviour across the organization, although such organizations might argue that they have a strong culture focused on 'individualism'.

For a first-runger, it is critical to understand the organizational culture from day one and learn to abide by the organizational norms within that culture. As Tom Brent of Disney puts it, senior executives value 'fit' with a company. For example, we discussed in Chapter 5 the importance of adopting the organization's communication culture to ensure an effective communication approach.

> It is critical to understand the organizational culture from day one and learn to abide by the organizational norms within that culture.

The factors that drive culture have been variously studied and documented, but for the purpose of first-rungers the focus here is on the following elements.

Organizational mission and values

The mission is the overarching 'reason to be' for an organization. Examples include aiming to achieve best customer satisfaction and highest share in a particular market, or to deliver the highest returns to shareholders. Many organizations have codified such organizational missions and sometimes have codified their values too. The importance of the mission and values to a first-runger, however, depends on how 'values-driven' the organization is. In highly values-driven organizations, modelling the values and aligning with the mission statement are important to demonstrate fit, even for first-rungers. For example, in my own experience as a management consultant, values were enormously important and everybody frequently referred to them for guidance and often used them as the basis for discussion where disagreement on the right course of action existed. In evaluations, alignment and adherence to values were also important factors in overall performance rankings. However, in less values-driven organizations, it is not as important for first-rungers to worry about organizational values.

Furthermore, just because an organization codifies its mission and values does not necessarily mean that it is highly values-driven. For example, one executive from a major investment bank recalls receiving a laminated page that espoused 10 values, such as 'We put clients first', that senior managers wanted everyone in the organization to adopt. However, according to the executive, the page came out of nowhere and was not only meaningless to most of the staff but was treated with derision because everyone already had their own way of doing things, and no one had ever talked about values beyond the need to be professional.

As a first-runger, you need to be attuned to the extent to which an organization is values-driven and pay attention to acting consistently with those values. Brian Murphy of Ericsson argues that seeing the bigger picture of the organization beyond the small scope of your specific role will help you achieve better 'fit'. Mary Peters of Microsoft suggests that one way to be consistent with values is to look for and emulate commonalities in how more senior employees act and talk. For example, despite any dress-code rules that exist in your office, if your bosses all wear formal business attire you would be advised to follow suit.

Evaluation and reward systems

When I was a second-year student at Princeton, I took a class in multi-variable calculus. For the first half of the semester, I barely opened the book and skipped most of the classes in favour of hitting the gym and courts to prepare for the tennis season. At mid-term, my over-reliance on the general intelligence that had got me through exams before became all too obvious, and I found myself earning a big fat juicy F on my mid-term examination. In the second half of the semester, I realized that there was no way I had time to run through the entire syllabus to catch up on what I had missed in the first half, so I decided that I would not worry about learning the subject per se, but I would focus entirely on learning what I needed to pass the final exam. I went to the mathematics department archives and found the last 10 years of final exam papers for my course. I went through each paper to understand the focus of the examinations. I discovered that there were always nine questions, and that seven out of those nine questions almost always came up (the remaining two showed no pattern). Of course, they were phrased differently and on the surface seemed like different questions, but in actual fact they required the application of the same set of mathematical principles each time. I then spent the bulk of my time on mastering these mathematical principles. By the time the exam came, I was able to finish all seven questions in half an hour, leaving two and a half hours to try to figure out the last two questions. I ended up getting an A minus on the final.

There were others on that course who I know learned more mathematics than I did in that semester but who did not do so well in the exam, not because they were any less intelligent but because they were less 'exam-smart'. They demonstrated a broader overall knowledge of the syllabus, but they did not have the same level of mastery as I had in the areas that clearly mattered most to the examiners.

When it comes to organizations, the equivalent of being exam-smart is being 'evaluation-smart'. If you understand what drives evaluations then you are well placed to ensure that you perform in the right areas to the right levels.

> The equivalent of being exam-smart is being 'evaluation-smart'. If you understand what drives evaluations then you are well placed to ensure that you perform in the right areas to the right levels.

For example, as every investment banker will attest, performing well on actual deals is what is most important for evaluation purposes. The same performance in non-deal-related work never counts as much.

Sometimes it is not even about performing highly in the right areas but merely about ticking some of the right boxes. For example, many organizations have components of their evaluations that include something around 'organization citizenship', covering contributions to the organization beyond the day-to-day demands of your job. It may include things like recruiting, organizing company events or sharing some new knowledge or best practice in a formal setting with colleagues. Ensuring that you do enough optically to tick these boxes is important. However, do not be fooled into thinking that ticking these evaluation boxes can compensate for underperformance in the core of your job.

Organizational structure and decision makers

The structure of organizations has a huge impact on culture. For example, one executive described her organization as having several divisions that, despite many necessary business linkages, operated almost independently. In her day-to-day job, she rarely had to interact with anyone outside her department. The decision maker was the head of the department and beneath him there was a clear hierarchy. Almost all decisions were made within the department, involving little communication with other parts of the organization. Within each department, loyalty was very high, and sometimes departments were even antagonistic towards each other. The consequence was that there was a differentiated culture across the organization by department that was largely set by the individuals running each department. When it came to evaluations, performance in the department and the views of the managers in that department were all that mattered.

For a first-runger in such an organization, it is important to understand that the department is effectively the organization and the norms set by the managers of that department, even if different to those of other parts of the organization, are the ones to emulate. Furthermore, you have to be careful about finding mentors outside your department, as this may raise issues of loyalty.

Other executives, such as Luis Costa of Procter & Gamble, detail organizations that are heavily interlinked across departments and divisions. They describe their day-to-day job as involving numerous interactions across different departments and divisions, eg product development, sales and marketing, and product management. Although within the department there was also a clear decision maker, most important decisions were driven by a consensus across the managers of the various departments. These organizations had a more universal culture that was not linked so closely to a few dominant individuals. Furthermore, when it came to evaluation, while the executives' department managers were still the most important contributors, managers and employees across other departments had meaningful influence too. For a first-runger in these types of organizations, it is important to recognize that you serve a much larger constituency than your own department and that individuals outside your core area critically input into your evaluations.

Role models and celebrated individuals

When I was conducting interviews, several executives spoke not only about what they felt had made them successful in their early careers but also about others in their organization whom they perceived to have been top performers. They frequently used the expression 'They were good' to describe these other top performers, and it reminded me of how often in my own career I had heard mention of those who are 'good'. Just as in the story in the Introduction, I was always fascinated by what made someone 'good', particularly in the eyes of others in an organization. In many ways, this book is a consequence of that fascination. Some organizations go one step further and actually celebrate individuals who are the best performers, with public mention, awards and prizes, and make role models of the best executives. For a first-runger, appreciating what makes the good 'good', and recognizing why certain individuals are celebrated and others are not, provides further insight into what the organization values most highly and is another way to get 'evaluation-smart'.

> Appreciating what makes the good 'good', and recognizing why certain individuals are celebrated and others are not, provides further insight into what the organization values most highly and is another way to get 'evaluation-smart'.

If you are attuned to your environment, it is not too difficult to observe these elements of culture at work and, while it may take a little longer to learn and adopt some of the more specific practices, you should be able to ensure that you 'fit' within the organization. However, you also have to see what is going on. In particular, there are two myths that are perpetuated in most organizations. These are the myths of non-hierarchy and meritocracy.

Myth 1: The myth of non-hierarchy

One of the evolutions in management philosophy that many organizations have adopted is a so-called 'flattening' of the organization. In other words, they have tried to remove layers of management and reduce hierarchy to liberate the potential of their workforce. Buzzwords such as 'empowerment', 'autonomy' and 'entrepreneurship' have permeated the management lexicon of even the most traditional and staid firms. Many firms even claim that they are non-hierarchical, period. However, while there is undoubtedly a whole spectrum of organizations with differing degrees of hierarchy, the only completely non-hierarchical organizations that I have ever heard of have workforces totalling one! There simply is no such thing as a truly non-hierarchical organization.

Jack Witherspoon of a top management consulting firm learned early on that his firm was far from being non-hierarchical. Jack once attended a meeting where the participants included four managing directors, three senior partners, two junior partners, two project managers and Jack, a first-year associate fresh out of business school. It turned out that Jack had actually been invited to this meeting by mistake: one of the project managers, with whom Jack had worked on a project at a former client's and who was unaware that the meeting was actually a high-level strategy meeting on how to restore the former major client relationship, had casually invited him along while passing in a corridor. Trying to be a good first-runger, Jack obeyed and turned up. He was a little more than surprised to discover the level of seniority of the meeting participants. They in turn were a little surprised at his attendance but, since he had been part of a working team with the former client, no one objected to his staying and nothing was mentioned.

During the course of the meeting, the managing directors and senior partners dominated the discussion, and Jack, knowing that the firm encouraged first-rungers to speak up, carefully chose one or two suitable opportunities to make minor contributions that the other meeting participants respectfully and patiently received. One of the points upon which everyone agreed was that a coherent strategy was required whereby the consulting team would assign responsibilities to cover specific divisions and specific people in the former client organization to try to restore the overall relationship. The meeting concluded with an exercise whereby the meeting chair, a senior partner, went round the table inviting the participants to indicate on which part of, and on whom in, the former client's organization they each wanted to focus. In turn, each participant around the table indicated his or her preferences until it was Jack's turn. Jack paused for a moment to contemplate his decision and then responded: 'I think I'll focus where I am told to focus.' Everyone laughed, and one of the managing directors responded by saying: 'You know what? Despite what they say about this being a non-hierarchical organization, that was a very good answer!'

My favourite example illustrating the true nature of hierarchy is about an investment bank where one analyst was in the office very late on a Friday night, staring down at a long weekend of work ahead of him. A phone rang and, because no one else was around, this analyst picked it up. It was someone from the New York office who was looking for help on a piece of work. When the analyst told this individual that there was no one available, the person from the New York office told the analyst that it was up to him to get the work done. The analyst explained that he was already working late and would have to work the entire weekend and could not possibly take on any more work. It was at this point that the New York individual decided that it was time to pull rank and asked the analyst if he knew who was making this request. The analyst replied that he did not know. The individual turned out to be a very senior New York managing director with a fearsome reputation, and he was adamant that the analyst did this work for him. On this occasion, and I certainly do not advise that you follow this path, the analyst responded by asking the senior managing director if he knew to whom *he* was speaking. When the managing director revealed that he had no idea, the analyst told him to get lost and promptly hung up. On this occasion, despite the best efforts of the managing director to find out who had been so outrageously defiant, the analyst's identity remained a secret even though the entire analyst class in London knew who he was.

Why is it important to recognize true hierarchy? It is important because, as a first-runger, you must understand and operate

> As a first-runger, you must understand and operate effectively within the boundaries of hierarchy.

effectively within the boundaries of hierarchy. A number of executives interviewed cited examples of first-rungers clearly overstepping their mark because they underappreciated boundaries. They thought their views, the views of employees with one or two years' experience, should receive as much 'airtime' as those of a 15-year veteran, or they acted without permission because they did not realize that they needed it, or they simply behaved too familiarly.

Myth 2: The myth of meritocracy

Almost all organizations believe themselves to be meritocratic. They typically claim that they reward, whether through compensation, promotion, responsibility or recognition, in commensurate proportion to the quality of job performance.

Meritocracy even features in many firms' codified values. However, it is a fallacy to believe that, if you enter any organization and outperform all of your peers, your superior performance alone will always secure your rapid and heralded progression through the firm's ranks.

> It is a fallacy to believe that, if you enter any organization and outperform all of your peers, your superior performance alone will always secure your rapid and heralded progression through the firm's ranks.

That is not to undermine the importance of performance and merit. It is, of course, crucial that you perform well and, while there are some executives who succeed solely through luck, these case are, fortunately, extremely rare. However, it comes back to the difference between good performers and good performers who also understand how to get ahead.

> It is, of course, crucial that you perform well... However, it comes back to the difference between good performers and good performers who also understand how to get ahead.

For a firm to be truly meritocratic, it must be able to rank its staff either numerically by merit or into sufficiently discrete and differentiated merit-based categories and reward the highest-ranked individuals commensurately. Many firms do actually rank their staff by class into numerical rankings, and the top performers usually receive higher pay and advance faster. However, to rank people in a truly meritocratic way, the organization must be able both to identify the relevant parameters of merit and to measure them accurately and consistently.

The first requirement most companies meet. The list of typical parameters should be unsurprising, given that many of their key components have featured heavily in this book:

- attitude and interpersonal skills;
- communication skills;
- functional skills, eg analytical and problem-solving skills;
- organizational citizenship, eg teamwork and cooperation;
- proactivity and entrepreneurship.

The second part is where it becomes impossible for any organization to be truly meritocratic. Measuring these parameters is not like determining the results in a 100-metre sprint where all observers can track the times and order of finishers and agree on the rank from the fastest to slowest runner within time ranges of remarkable accuracy. The process by which almost all of these evaluation parameters are measured is inherently subjective because the parameters are largely qualitative – how exactly, for example, do you decide that one person is a better communicator than another person? Sometimes it is obvious, but often it is not. A subjective process of evaluating qualitative parameters leads to two problems in establishing rank.

Firstly, a subjective evaluation process is subject to both intentional and unintentional bias. Intentional bias is explicit prejudice such as when evaluators knowingly give the best reviews to those whom they like most rather than to those who have performed best. Unintentional bias is when evaluators subconsciously give the best reviews to those individuals who most resemble them, whether it is in style, cultural background or general approach.

Secondly, a subjective evaluation process causes further variation when there is more than one evaluator. Even with the best of intentions and mostly tightly defined metrics, no two evaluators will always share the same view. I have seen this most clearly when discussing new recruits' performance in the interview process. Interviewers frequently disagree about whether individuals should be hired. Similarly, a class of executives in a firm evaluated along the same metrics but by a number of different evaluators inevitably results in some candidates receiving more favourable reviews than others based solely on the fact that they had different evaluators.

> I have seen many first-rungers who were genuinely very strong performers become disillusioned, having been put back in their place after unknowingly overstepping their bounds.

Why is it important to understand these two myths? It is important because you need to set your expectations realistically. I have seen many first-rungers who were genuinely very strong performers become disillusioned, having been put back in their place after unknowingly overstepping their bounds. I have seen the same first-rungers and others come out of review sessions feeling let down and unsure why someone was being promoted ahead of them because they did not appreciate that the promoted person had the support of a very influential mentor or was actually being rewarded for doing a decent job on the most important project – the 'pet project', as Maria Liston of Sun Microsystems calls it. Often this frustration gets to them and breeds cynicism and actually affects their ability to succeed. If you can see past these two myths and maintain enough self-confidence, you can ride out any short-term fluctuations in chance and position yourself to maximize your chances of rapid success.

Handling politics for first-rungers

Most of the executives interviewed felt that understanding politics was important, but were far less

> The advice that most executives give is to try to avoid politics.

comfortable recommending any real political actions for first-rungers. On the whole, they felt that there was more downside than upside in actually getting involved. The advice that most executives give is to try to avoid politics. One of the benefits of being a first-runger is that you can, by keeping your head down, largely avoid having to deal with politics. Politics tends to occur higher up the organization, for example where there are power struggles and competition for resources, and consequently first-rungers do not feature.

While politics is a greater focus for more seasoned executives than for first-rungers, you would still do well to abide by five principles to prevent suffering any political fallout and to further your chances of being successful.

Ensure you have a no-enemy policy

The first and by far the most important principle is not to create any enemies. This may seem true for executives at all levels, but the reality is that, as executives become more senior, in some organizations they may have to choose sides in power struggles or when disagreements on major issues occur. By so doing, they cannot help but make enemies as a consequence of an 'if not with us, then against us' mentality. First-rungers have the luxury of not having to choose sides, as they naturally fall into one camp by direct association with their bosses.

There is no secret to not making enemies. Sometimes, it requires that you bite your tongue when you want to answer back. Sometimes, it requires that you do some work that you would prefer not to do. In general, however, it requires that you always cooperate, never argue and maintain high levels of tolerance.

Put up with it or escape through 'pull'

Conflict management is connected to the no-enemy policy, in that the best way to manage conflict is to avoid it. Sometimes, how-

> The best way to manage conflict is to avoid it.

ever, conflict can be difficult to avoid. For example, you might be in a position where you are assigned to a highly unpleasant piece of work with a highly micromanaging and generally unpleasant boss. You might well feel strongly inclined to resist your boss and try to curb his or her micromanaging tendencies. In such a situation, however, the best thing you can do is put up with it and seek to work around the problem by being extra proactive and trying to keep your boss too busy to micromanage you. There is no secret to making your life any easier, but there is simply little upside to precipitating conflict. A number of executives spoke of highly unpleasant episodes in their careers that they took on the chin before moving on.

If you must take action to escape from an unpleasant assignment or avoid getting involved in the first place, there is one general principle that you should observe. Always try to negotiate into an alternative assignment rather than out of an existing one. The difference in positioning is critical. Recall Chapter 1 on attitude, which included the advice that you should never complain. If you focus on the reasons why you want out, you have to concentrate on negatives – the project lacks certain dimensions, the hours are long, the boss is unpleasant etc. You are effectively complaining. However, if you focus on trying to get into another assignment, you can accentuate positives – the project work is particularly exciting, you always wanted to work in this area, you would love to get some exposure to different managers etc. The best outcome is if you can create 'pull' from another assignment, in other words find another senior manager to 'pull' you on to his or her project.

Of course, if you are already on an existing project, you have to consider the appropriate time to make your move. For some projects, there is no way to escape and you are back to the 'put up with it' approach.

Look for the right place at the right time

Much of being highly successful, and this becomes more true as you proceed through your career, is being in the right place at the right time. If you are a fantastically high performer but in the wrong part of an organization, you are unlikely to do as well as if you were in the right part of the organization.

> Much of being highly successful, and this becomes more true as you proceed through your career, is being in the right place at the right time.

Brian Murphy of Ericsson is a good example of someone who recognized and actively sought the best opportunities. For the first year of his time at Ericsson, Brian worked in a product area that was on the ninth release of its core product. Brian saw that the improvement from version to version was becoming increasingly marginal. He recognized that there was little upside in continuing to work on this product in an organization that he knew from the culture was focused on innovation. Instead, he looked around the organization for another product area that was focused on innovative and cutting-edge technology. There were a number of areas focused on new technologies. However, Brian also recognized that many early-stage technologies did not progress past the initial research phase and was a little more refined in his search. He found a perfect fit in an area focused on a new product development based in California. This business unit had been up and running for a while, and its new product continued to show promising potential. Brian successfully negotiated 'pull' to this product area and, through his contributions to a successful and innovative product development effort, his internal reputation was far more greatly enhanced than it would have been by working on subsequent releases in his original product area.

Spotting the right place and knowing the right time stem in part from understanding the culture of the organization, specifically what the organization most values. For example, the organization might value innovation highly, like Ericsson; it might value the largest cash flow-generating part of the business; it might be focused on the fastest-growing businesses; or it might be dominated by a particular business line or geographic region. Whatever the answer, the areas most valued by the organization are where you want to try to be. Timing also matters. For example, an organization may value most highly the fastest-growing businesses, but only after they have shown a consistent track record of fast growth over three years.

> Without forging overt alliances and playing politics, smart first-rungers recognize who in the organization are going places and try to find ways of working with them.

A second element to being in the right place at the right time is working with the right people. Without forging overt alliances and playing politics, smart first-rungers recognize who in the organization are going places and try to find ways of working with them. Even if you do not develop mentoring relationships, simply being part of a high-performing team, under a highly regarded boss, will improve your overall reputation through a 'halo' effect.

Remember that you are always on show

One of the key dimensions of being professional is behaving and acting appropriately at all times – not just in the office, but also in social situations with your work colleagues and bosses. After a while, you will develop a level of comfort with colleagues and bosses at work, and it is easy to let your guard down. I have seen colleagues at Christmas parties get so drunk that they utterly embarrassed themselves. The lesson to remember is that every interaction is important and you must always put your best side across. This does not mean that you have to be boring, but it does mean that you always maintain control and definitely never cross the line of unprofessional behaviour even in a non-professional environment.

Do not expect recognition and appreciation for your efforts and do not always trust it when you get it

Human nature is such that we all like to be recognized and appreciated. The best managers and executives at all levels of the career ladder show genuine recognition and appreciation for effort and for good work because they recognize the benefits of positive reinforcement and encouragement. Many managers and executives, though, are less forthright with their praise, not because they think you have not done a decent job and not because they are bad managers or executives, but often because they just do not think about it. Do not make the mistake of expecting appreciation and becoming disillusioned when it does not come. If you are worried about whether you have done a good job, ask for feedback and do so, as we discussed in Chapter 8, with specific questions, not a generalized 'How am I doing?'

Most dangerous of all are those gutless managers and executives who tell their subordinates that they are doing fine, only to nail them in their reviews or criticize them to their colleagues. There is little you can do to combat this other than delivering great work, but as a general rule you should treat all praise and appreciation with a certain degree of scepticism and focus only on continuing to improve.

Controlling perception by building a personal brand

One of the most telling findings from the research was the importance executives gave to perception. Nearly a third of executives surveyed felt that how first-rungers were perceived was as important as their actual performance, if not more important. This is strong evidence of the myth of meritocracy but, if you think about it, the world is full of evidence of the importance of perception. Walk into any chemist's, look at the price of well-known painkillers and compare them with a generic ibuprofen product. The well-known painkillers command a substantial premium over the generic one despite the fact that the two products are chemically virtually identical. The difference is perception – also known as 'brand'.

So important is brand in the business world that most branded products have dedicated 'brand managers' whose responsibilities are to manage the value of the brand and ensure that it sustains a price premium in the marketplace. The rest of this chapter is about looking at your own personal brand and trying to maximize its value; in other words, it is about creating positive perceptions.

In Chapter 1, I discussed the importance of self-awareness and self-mastery as a keystone of success. Self-awareness and self-mastery, however, are both inward-looking. They are about looking at yourself and making real changes. When it comes to managing perception, you need to be outward-looking. You need to understand how others respond to you and perceive you, and you need to make sure that your presence, behaviour and performance all drive positive perceptions.

It is critical that you note that all of the advice and lessons in this book are essential to driving perception. It is very hard to create a perception that has no foundation in reality. Your personal brand

It is critical that you note that all of the advice and lessons in this book are essential to driving perception. It is very hard to create a perception that has no foundation in reality.

needs to be underpinned by a great attitude, quality skills and a strong support group in the form of your network and personal mentors.

While perception is important on an ongoing basis, at no point is it more important than in first impressions. Even before you do a single piece of work, your bosses and colleagues will have formed a view of you from their first impressions. They will also have formed expectations about how you are likely to work, based on what in truth is scant evidence. The thing about expectations is that, once they are formed, people naturally look for evidence to support them. If your bosses gain an impression that you are sloppy and chaotic, they will be more likely to notice any sloppiness in your work than if their initial impression is that you are on top of things. People have a very hard time changing their minds.

When it comes to developing and managing your personal brand, you need to ask yourself what you want your personal brand to portray. The answer is tricky. The research for this book

The best first-rungers are all-rounders... However, when it comes to building a personal brand, you need to demonstrate particular distinctiveness in one or two areas.

has led me to believe that the best first-rungers are all-rounders. In other words, they demonstrate strong capabilities in all areas. However, when it comes to building a personal brand, you need to demonstrate particular distinctiveness in one or two areas above and beyond your well-rounded overall capabilities. David Beckham, the famous English football (soccer) captain, is a great all-round footballer, but he is most frequently remembered as one of the greatest all-time players at taking free kicks and crosses. Even his advertisements for the sporting goods company Adidas focus on him practising free kicks. When it comes to thinking about your personal brand, you need to think of those one or two areas that you can excel in and that will differentiate you. Nine types of personal brands that many executives have encountered in their organizations are briefly described below:

1. **The 'quant'.** Quants are masters at quantitative analysis. They understand spreadsheets inside out and can break down any problem and build the most fantastic models. They are sought after whenever business problems involve quantitative analysis and modelling.
2. **The 'computer whizz'.** The computer whizz has a deep understanding of the workings of computers and the main programs. While many organizations have their own IT departments, there is usually someone in the main business area who can solve most problems as they come up. Such a person is in heavy demand for business problems with significant IT components.
3. **The 'hard worker'.** Hard workers demonstrate unwavering commitment and are willing and able to work both at higher intensity levels and for longer than most. They are valued because they are always available and always contributing.
4. **The 'team player'.** Most businesses organize themselves in teams at various levels within the organization. Team players are highly regarded because they always seem to put the team before their own needs and because they create an upbeat, productive and enjoyable team environment. They are valued simply because they are great to work with.
5. **The 'communicator'.** Some executives are superb at communicating. They speak clearly and crisply, and command attention. They are able to synthesize complex problems and explain them easily and quickly. Senior managers like them because they come across very well and professionally.
6. **The 'networker'.** Networkers seem to know everyone and have great word-of-mouth reputations. They are social, well liked and often charismatic. Senior managers value them because they exhibit strong people skills.
7. **The 'organizer'.** Organizers are great at organizing meetings, events or conferences. They have a knack of being able to manage many moving parts and keep things running smoothly. Organizers are highly valued because they manage to put together events seemingly effortlessly without any major problems.
8. **The 'entertainer'.** As with team players, entertainers are great to have around because they create an environment that is fun and enjoyable whether in a team context or not. They are great in front of clients and senior managers because they have a great sense of

humour and have a way of lifting moods. Unlike 'class clowns', however, entertainers are not disruptive and are not more focused on telling jokes than doing work. Instead, their sense of humour is well timed, and they successfully balance injecting fun into proceedings with getting on with necessary work.

9. **The 'creative'.** Particularly in organizations that require some degree of creativity, for example sales- and marketing-orientated companies or companies geared towards innovation, there are usually executives who are highly regarded for their ability to think creatively or 'out of the box'. They are attractive to managers because they progress problem solving and contribute greatly to innovation.

While these nine personal first-rung brands are relatively common, you should not feel that you have to fit precisely into any one of these categories. You do need to figure out, however, where your greatest strengths lie and develop your personal brand around them.

General principles of managing perception

Regardless of what your personal brand is, there are also certain principles that you should heed in managing some very basis tenets of perception, particularly when dealing with people for the first time.

Speak crisply and with confidence
With two chapters focused on communication in this book, it should be no surprise that how you speak has a marked impact on how others regard you. From your choice of words to the tone of your voice, how you speak is, in fact, one of the strongest drivers of perception and is well worth considerable attention for improvement.

Exhibit positive body language
There are numerous statistics about how the majority of communication is non-verbal – I have seen ranges from 60 to 90 per cent. I do not know which are the correct figures, but certainly your body language conveys much about you. Confidence, enthusiasm and

> Confidence, enthusiasm and alertness... are all highly visible in your posture, in the set of your face and in your eyes and general demeanour.

alertness, for example, are all highly visible in your posture, in the set of your face and in your eyes and general demeanour. Individuals who slouch, have dull expressions or make little eye contact make negative impressions. Your body language is a reflection of your underlying attitude and mood and of habit. If you have a good attitude and ensure an upbeat mood, you will naturally reflect positive body language. With respect to habit, it is to be hoped that you listened to the nagging of your parents while growing up – stand up straight, do not straggle when walking, look people in the eye, offer a firm hand when shaking hands etc – and have already developed these good habits. If this is not the case, you need to develop them.

Dress sensibly

In many ways, dress sense is an extension of body language. However, such is the variation in different organizations on dress codes that it is inappropriate to prescribe any particular mode of dress. Suffice it to say, however, that you should be dressed appropriately. Regardless of the dress code, in an office environment you should wear clean and pressed clothes and polished shoes. I know of many examples of first-rungers who have been 'dressed down' for inappropriate dress – including one colleague who in two consecutive reviews was evaluated negatively for dressing like an absent-minded professor! I have personally always abided by the principle of emulating the senior managers. If your bosses wear formal business attire, then so should you.

Be on time

You do not have to be present for people to form their first impression of you. If your first interaction with someone new is being late, that person will already be forming a negative first impression of you. It is a basic courtesy and a mark of professionalism to be on time and, particularly with people whom you have never met before, there is no excuse for lateness.

Maintain good personal hygiene

Yes, we are getting down to basics here, but you would be surprised at how many people have poor personal hygiene. There is nothing more to say except that you must ensure you are clean, shower daily with soap (and if you are male shave), wear a suitable deodorant (but do not overdo the perfume or cologne), sport a conservative haircut and keep clean and neat fingernails.

In a nutshell – How to be politically savvy

- Understand your organization's culture.

- Do not fall for the myths of non-hierarchy and meritocracy.

- Ensure a no-enemy policy.

- Be prepared to put up with your situation or escape conflict through 'pull' from other projects.

- Look for the right place at the right time.

- Remember that you are always on show.

- Do not expect recognition and appreciation for your efforts and do not always trust it when you get it.

- Control perception and build a personal brand:

  - Speak crisply and with confidence.

  - Exhibit positive body language.

  - Dress sensibly.

Conclusion

This book has been about what it takes to succeed on the first rung of the career ladder. It is most relevant for business environments because most (but not all) of the research was drawn from business executives and because my own experience and perspectives are drawn from a business environment. However, I firmly believe that the principles in this book hold for any first-runger aspiring to succeed in any organization with a career structure, whether it is in the private or the public sector. The findings have been given to you straight, and I believe that the advice in this book is accurate. Most of the advice is also only going to help you – learning to become an efficient researcher or finding mentors has little downside. However, some advice, in particular around 'ensuring a relentless work ethic', does come with a potential downside in the context of your overall life.

All careers require that you work hard, and most people whom I have seen performing well have generally enjoyed applying themselves. However, some careers are particularly demanding, and you have to make significant personal sacrifices to perform and deliver as required to get ahead. These types of careers are not for all. Having worked in two of the most gruelling industries in front-line roles, I have witnessed marriages break down, I have seen stress beating people into the ground emotionally and on occasion even sending them to hospital, and I have watched people become desperately unhappy as their personal lives suffered. These people have gone through these experiences despite the fact that they were frequently star performers. At the same time, I have seen others in these industries quite content to work 80- or 90-hour weeks on difficult projects with difficult people because the goal of succeeding in their careers was important enough to them to warrant the sacrifice.

Kim Clark, the former dean of Harvard Business School, used to say annually to the graduating class of MBA students, 'No success in the workplace can compensate for failure at home.' He would say this twice over, such was his conviction in this belief. It is one that I personally share, but it may not be true for all. For some people, career success may be more important than a happy family or social life.

The only advice I can give you is to recognize that you have to make trade-offs. You cannot always have it all. One of the pieces of advice we discussed in 'managing upwards' was around managing the expectations of your bosses. You also need to manage your own expectations. You might decide that you are going to limit your working week to 50 hours because that would allow you to maintain important personal relationships. However, you cannot expect to be the best first-runger while working a 50-hour week when the other first-rungers are working 60 hours. If you do not recognize this trade-off and do not explicitly choose to make it, you will only become frustrated and disappointed when you see others progress faster.

I am also aware that there are two subjects that come up in many business books that I have not discussed in this book. These subjects are ethics and leadership, and there are good reasons why I have not ostensibly spent any time on them.

Ethics

A question that I like to ask when I discuss ethics in business or politics is this: 'Do you believe it is possible for people to reach the top, for example to be the CEO of a major company or organization, or be president or prime minister of a nation, and be able to look their mother in the eye and say that they have done nothing along the way that would make her ashamed?' The almost unanimous answer I get is negative, and the reason people give is that getting ahead requires you to compromise your integrity because you have to say, or do, or not say, or not do things that you believe are right in order to please the powers that control your path to the top. They believe that things like duplicity, character assassination, taking personal credit when not due, not sticking up for someone when appropriate and passing blame when unwarranted go on all the time at the top echelons of organizations.

Thankfully, few executives believe that you need to compromise your ethics to succeed on the first rung. The main reason is that advancement on and from the first rung is much less about competing against specific people than it is about performing well and being visible to the people who matter. As you move up the career ladder towards the top of the 'pyramid', you come into more direct competition with colleagues and this is where far greater pressure exists to compromise your ethics. So, fortunately, it is a subject that I have been able largely to avoid in this book. I am grateful, because ethics has become a hot topic of late, with the subject making headlines and even increasing in importance in business school curricula, and it is a subject that I would struggle to further. To me, ethics has always been very simple. We each have a conscience that tells us the truth on these matters. Deep down, you know if something is unethical, and you choose either to be consistent with your ethics – to act or speak with integrity – or not.

Leadership

One of the things that you will note from the recruiting brochures of many companies and organizations, and business and other professional schools is the importance they place on so-called leadership skills in their new recruits. Leadership has even spawned an industry unto itself with hundreds of books on the subject. Why then have I not spent any time talking about being a leader?

The answer is that I *have* talked about leadership, but I have not marketed it as such. When I advised you to 'take ownership' of projects, that was about leadership. When I introduced the concept of 'quiet management', that was about leadership. When I talked about the different dimensions of having a great attitude, that too was about leadership. The real question is: why have I not packaged them as leadership skills, as is currently in vogue?

The answer is down to an argument I made in an article that I wrote as a student at Harvard Business School for the school newspaper, the *Harbus*. The article was about why Harvard Business School students and alumni were sometimes viewed as arrogant. One of the reasons, I wrote, was because, from the first day that they arrive on campus, students are instilled with a sense that they are 'future leaders' and 'shapers of society' through the faculty, the administration and the companies and organizations that recruit there. I went on to say that, while most

Harvard Business School graduates are typically impressive people and have been outstanding performers on the first rung, they are actually still in relatively junior jobs when they leave business school, jobs that I would even still class as first-rung jobs. Most have no management responsibilities, and those who do have a handful of team members only. They are certainly not yet 'shapers of society'.

I did not want to package certain skills or attributes as part of leadership in this book because the skills and attributes themselves are what is important, and calling them 'leadership skills' is spin (and potentially detrimental spin at that). The reality of the first-rung job is that you have to do a lot more following than you do leading. If you walk in and believe you are there as a leader in any grand sense of the term, you will lose sight of the reality of your environment, an environment with boundaries and hierarchies that you have to observe and obey.

I said in the Introduction that I would have benefited enormously from reading a book like this when I was starting my career. I would also have benefited enormously from reading such a book after graduating from business school, and I firmly believe that this book is as useful for newly minted MBAs as it is for first-degree graduates.

If truth be told, much of the advice in this book is still relevant for me as I journey through the middle rungs of my career, and I plan to refer back to it many times for advice despite the fact that I have written it. I hope that it will not be a book that you will read once and put away only to gather dust. Certainly, some of the tips, tricks and rules of thumb are worthy of reference, particularly in the middle section of the book, but beyond these I hope you will revisit other parts of the book to learn afresh more of its lessons.

The basics of spreadsheets

Key elements of spreadsheet functionality for analysis

■ **Cell references.** Rows are numbered up and down the page; columns are lettered from left to right. Therefore every cell is uniquely identified by a letter and a number, eg A1, H543. In fact, the most common spreadsheet program, Microsoft Excel, has 256 columns (A to IV) and 65,536 rows per worksheet, giving you 16,777,216 cells with which to work.

■ **Data series.** Terminology to describe data organized in a row or a column.

■ **Data array.** Terminology to describe data organized across both rows and columns. For example, suppose you are recording the examination results of 30 students in each of 10 different subjects. You would probably have an array with 31 rows and 11 columns of data including title rows and columns.

■ **Formula bar.** At the top of the grid of cells is a formula bar. You can type formulae either directly into the cell or into the formula bar, but the latter is easier to use, particularly for longer formulae.

■ **Formulae and basic notation:**[1]
  – All formulae begin with '=', eg =A1+A2.
  – Separate arguments in cell formulae with ',', eg =SUM(A1,A3, A8).

- Describe series and arrays with ':', eg the series (A1:A10) or the array (A1:B25). The array (A1:IV65536) describes an array containing every cell in a spreadsheet.

■ **Hard-wiring cells.** Typing numbers directly into a cell formula, which therefore do not change unless you retype the numbers.

■ **Linking cells.** Linking a cell formula with the output of another cell (which may be hard-wired or linked itself). You can link cells within a worksheet, between worksheets and even between different spreadsheet files.

■ **Relative versus absolute cell references.** Spreadsheets default to relative references. If cell A1 has a formula that sums the output of cells B1 and C1 using relative references, and you copy this formula to cell A2, the formula in cell A2 will automatically sum the output of cells B2 and C2. If you used absolute references, the formula in cell A2 would be identical to A1 and also sum B1 and C1. You should be able to mix absolute and relative references in formulae, and you can fix either or both of the dimensions of the cell references, eg the lettered column and/or the numbered rows.

■ **Basic arithmetic notation.** In cell formulae, most are the same as in everyday use, but some are different, eg multiplying and exponentiating (raising to a power):
  - Add: '+'
  - Subtract: '-'
  - Multiply: '*'
  - Divide: '/'
  - Power: '^'

■ **Use of parentheses (brackets) to control hierarchy of arithmetic functions.** For example, =5+(4*3), which equals 17, is not the same as =(5+4)*3, which equals 27, because the spreadsheet calculates within the parentheses first. Parentheses can also be nested, eg =(10*(5*(8-3)))+(6/(10-8)) will calculate out to 280.

■ **Copy, cut and paste functions.** Use to reproduce formulae in different cells. Copy and paste defaults to relative references unless the formula is fixed, while cut and paste retains the precise original formula, as it actually moves the contents from one cell to another.

■ **Drag and drop.** Use with a mouse or through the menus to extend a series, eg if you type 'January' and 'February' into cells A1 and A2, highlight the two cells and left-click on the bottom corner until you get a solid cross shape and holding down the left-click drag and drop down to cell A12, the series of data will recognize the months and fill them out for you.

Key elements of spreadsheet functionality for formatting

■ **Formatting quantitative output of cells.** Know how to change the units and decimal points for cells, eg different currencies, percentages, and number of decimal points.

■ **Formatting text output of cells.** Just as in a text document, know how to change font type, size, colour and style (italics, bold, underline).

■ **Inserting/deleting cells, rows and columns.** Sometimes empty cells, rows and columns enhance presentation. Be careful, however, that introducing empty cells, rows and columns does not make it harder to do quick drag and drops.

■ **Labelling worksheets.** Open up a work book and the default mode is three spreadsheets, each of which you should know how to label.

■ **Inserting/deleting worksheets.** Sometimes you need more than three spreadsheets. Models can grow to contain hundreds of worksheets.

■ **Moving worksheets.** Multiple spreadsheets in a workbook often need to be sequenced in some kind of logical order; know how to move spreadsheets to change their order.

■ **Using print preview and page set-up.** Know how to organize the visual display of your spreadsheets so that they appear clear and well structured when you print.

■ **Splitting windows.** When your spreadsheets are large, you may want to have several views of the spreadsheet. This requires you to know how to 'split windows', which you can do along both the horizontal and vertical axes.

■ **Freezing panes.** Every spreadsheet should be organized by labelled rows and labelled columns, eg financial spreadsheets are organized in rows by time units, such as months or years, and in columns by line items, such as revenues, costs and profits. If your spreadsheets are large, you have to 'freeze' the labelled rows and columns so that you can tell what the content of a cell in the middle of the spreadsheet represents.

■ **Creating and formatting charts.** Most data are best displayed not through tables of numbers, but through charts that visually demonstrate the key relationships, trends and messages within the numbers. Spreadsheets include a charting function, which includes many different types of charts from pie charts to scatter plots to column charts. The 'ChartWizard' is a very user-friendly step-by-step tool that you should use to create charts – it is usually a small column graph icon in the row of buttons on the top of your spreadsheet screen. Using ChartWizard, you should learn to choose the appropriate chart and how to format it, including how to: create titles and label axes; adjust scale; colour/shade data points/lines/columns/bars/segments; and format data labels.

The 10 most commonly used mathematics and statistics spreadsheet functions

1. **SUM** – calculates the sum (of a series of data).
2. **AVERAGE** – calculates the mean.
3. **MEDIAN** – calculates the median.
4. **MODE** – calculates the mode.
5. **MAX** – calculates the maximum number.
6. **MIN** – calculates the minimum number.
7. **SUMPRODUCT** – sums up the products of several series of data.
8. **COUNT** – calculates the number of entries in a series.
9. **STDEV** – calculates the standard deviation.
10. **CORREL** – calculates the correlation coefficient between two sets of data.

Note

1   Where ' ' is written, this highlights the contents as the notation. In other words, ' ' is not part of the notation.

Research approach and details

Research approach

Hundreds of executives participated in the research for this book through a formal survey, structured interviews, e-mail exchanges and more informal conversations. The formal survey used a proprietary market research technology, a 'Brainjuicer',[1] to assess the most important themes for success in respondents' early careers. These survey themes formed the basis of the main themes and topics in *From New Recruit to High Flyer*. Deep structured interviews provided much of the detail on each of the main themes and topics, and real-life illustrative examples and cases from a number of different executives at different companies. On specific topics, a number of executives were kind enough to share their thoughts through numerous e-mail exchanges. Finally, informal conversations with colleagues, clients, classmates and friends over lunch, drinks or dinner have proved an unexpected source of great material.

Research details

■ Table A.1 shows the full list of organizations where research participants have worked. Not all participants are directly quoted or
referred to in the book, but they were all important contributors
to the key messages.
■ Figure A.1 shows the split of research participants between the
United States, Europe, Asia and the rest of the world.

■ Figure A.2 shows the split of research participants across the type of organization/industry where they have worked.

Table A.1 *Organizations where research participants have worked[1]*

Organization[2,3]	Type of organization
ABB	Industrial
Accenture	Management consulting
Adroit Systems	Engineering
Aerospace Corp	Engineering
AirTouch	Telecoms
Allied Irish Bank	Banking
Alok Industries	Conglomerate
American Express	General finance
American Medical Security	Insurance
Ameritech	Telecoms
Apax Partners	Private equity
Aramark	Food services
Arthur Andersen	Accounting
AT&T	Telecoms
AT Kearney	Management consulting
Bain & Company	Management consulting
Bain Capital	Private equity
Bank of America Securities	Private equity
Boston Consulting Group	Management consulting
Bear Stearns	Investment banking
Bell Canada	Telecoms
Bertelsmann	Media
Blackstone	Private equity
Booz Allen Hamilton	Management consulting
British Airways	Airlines
Cap Gemini	Conglomerate
Celanese	Engineering
Chase Capital	Private equity
Cheney Communication	Telecoms
Chiron	Biotechnology
Chrysler	Automobiles
Citigroup	Banking
CitySearch	Other
Clear Channel Communications	Telecoms

Table A.1 *Organizations where research participants have worked[1]* (Continued)

Organization[2,3]	Type of organization
Constellation Energy	Energy
Cover Girl	Retail
Credit Suisse First Boston	Investment banking
Cunningham and Walsh	Law
Cypress Group	Private equity
DeanWitter	Banking
Dell	Technology
Deloitte Consulting	Management consulting
Deutsche Bank	Investment banking
Disney	Media
Donaldson, Lufkin & Jenrette	Investment banking
Dow Chemical	Chemicals
Drumtight Painting	Industrial
Eli Lilly	Pharmaceutical
EnGene	Biotechnology
Enron	Energy
Enterprise Oil	Energy
Ericsson	Telecoms
Ernst & Young	Accounting
Estee Lauder	Retail
Fidelity	Investment management
Ford	Automobiles
Fuji Bank	Banking
General Electric	Conglomerate
General Motors	Automobiles
GlaxoSmithKline	Pharmaceutical
Goldman Sachs	Investment banking
Google	Technology
Greenwich Associates	Management consulting
Hatch Engineering	Engineering
Hewlett-Packard	Technology
Honeywell	Conglomerate
Intel	Technology
Intuit	Technology
Invesco	Investment management
JP Morgan	Investment banking

Table A.1 *Organizations where research participants have worked[1]* *(Continued)*

Organization[2,3]	Type of organization
Juroku Banking Corp	Investment banking
Kaplan	Education
KPMG	Accounting
Lazard Freres	Investment banking
Lehman Brothers	Investment banking
McKinsey & Company	Management consulting
McMaster-Carr	Industrial
Marakon Consulting	Management consulting
Match.com	Other
Mercer Consulting	Management consulting
Merrill Lynch	Investment banking
Microsoft	Technology
Mitchell Madison Group	Management consulting
Mitsubishi	Conglomerate
Montgomery Securities	Investment banking
Morgan Stanley	Investment banking
NBC	Media
Nortel Networks	Technology
Novartis	Pharmaceutical
Oppenheimer	Investment banking
Oracle	Technology
Orange	Telecoms
PaineWebber	Investment banking
Panasonic	Technology
Pepsi-Cola	Retail
Permira	Private equity
Procter & Gamble	Consumer goods
Putnam	Investment management
PricewaterhouseCoopers	Accounting
Qantas	Airlines
Radisson	Hotelier
Ralph Lauren	Retail
Reebok	Retail
Reuters	Technology
Roland Berger	Management consulting

Table A.1 *Organizations where research participants have worked[1]*
(Continued)

Organization[2,3]	Type of organization
Sabena	Airlines
Salomon Brothers	Investment banking
Schlumberger	Engineering
Schroders	Investment banking
Shell	Energy
Siebel Systems	Technology
Siemens	Conglomerate
Skadden Arps	Law
Sony	Conglomerate
Starwood Resorts	Hotelier
Sun Microsystems	Technology
Telefonica	Telecoms
Teligent	Telecoms
Texaco	Energy
Ticketmaster	Media
Towers Perrin	Management consulting
Twentieth Century Fox	Media
Unisys	Technology
United Nations	Public sector
Universal Studios	Media
USAID	Public sector
US House of Representatives	Public sector
US Robotics	Technology
Value Partners	Management consulting
Warburg Pincus	Private equity
Wasserstein Perella & Co	Investment banking
World Bank	Banking
Xerox	Technology

Notes:

[1] Research participants include survey respondents, interviewees and other participants.

[2] In some cases, executives have worked at more than one organization; in other cases, more than one executive has worked at the same company.

[3] Some organizations no longer exist in the form of the entities listed here because of mergers, acquisitions etc.

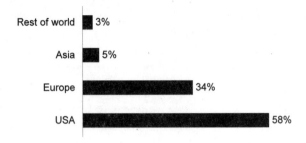

Figure A.1 *Geographical breakdown of where research participants have worked*

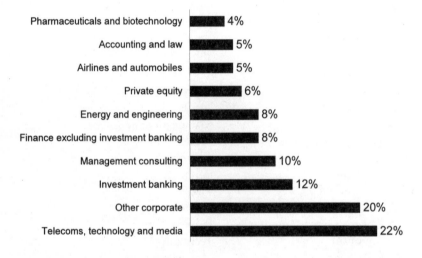

Figure A.2 *Industry breakdown of where research participants have worked*

Note

1   For more information on the company that owns this proprietary technology, see http://www.brainjuicer.com/.